Speaking American English Well

Dina Dahbany-Miraglia
Queensborough Community College CUNY

KENDALL/HUNT PUBLISHING COMPANY
4050 Westmark Drive Dubuque, Iowa 52002

There are 5 audio tapes (about 400 minutes). Every exercise in the text is verbalized. These tapes can be used for self-study or for classroom/lab instruction. © 1998 Dina Dahbany-Miraglia, the tapes may be purchased directly from the author at

Mailing Address	or	E-Mail Address
P.O. Box 864		ddmqcc@worldnet.att.net
Flushing, NY 11354-0864		

ISBN 0-7872-5431-2

Printed in the United States of America
10 9 8 7 6 5 4 3 2 1

Contents

List of Figures

List of Tables

Preface

This text is the result of fifteen years of teaching English as a Second Language: reading, writing and speech, and three years of testing this textbook in the ESL classroom. It comes out of a need to be able to teach ESL speech, voice and diction, and conversation courses with a single text and a minimum of handouts.

To help students work on the difficulties they have speaking English necessitates teaching English phonemics. The 41 distinct phonemes plus a lack of congruence between pronunciation and spelling, complicates teaching English speech.

Whether in high school or in college, ESL and other speech students are also struggling with learning a lot of vocabulary within a relatively short time. This textbook includes vocabulary along with phonemic representations and definitions.

And we have to deal with the problems of boredom and frustration.

Drills are still one of the more effective techniques for teaching articulation. What I have done is avoid relying on single-word and single-phrase drills. Instead I have incorporated all sorts of rhymes, riddles, and a few songs and dialogues, each keyed to specific sounds and combinations of sounds.

The dialogues are conversational in style. The various rhymes derive from several literary genres. These can be helpful for high school and college students who are or will be taking basic literature courses.

No book of any kind is completed in a vacuum. The initial stimuli were Irene Alterbaum and Joyce Buck whose LISTENSPEAK showed me the way. I am grateful for the guidance of my editors, and for the insight and depth of knowledge of my copy editors Moya Phillips and Sherry Gillman-Rada. For the audio technical support I am lucky to have the advice of Ronaldo Carter and John Funke.

To my chair Lee Pavés, as always, gratitude for your guidance and support. To Steven Kutyna, my rock, my love.

CHAPTER I

How to Use This Text

INTRODUCTION

This text is a workbook designed to help high school and college students who are speakers of ENGLISH DIALECTS learn to SPEAK AMERICAN ENGLISH WELL. Students who are shoring up their reading and writing skills in English will also find this volume useful.

Although the emphasis here is on clarity of speech, one cannot learn to speak a language well through pronunciation drills alone.

The various exercises in this text: drills, doggerels, rhymes, riddles, songs and dialogues, are supplemented by sections explaining the patterns specific to several pronunciation:spelling problems, such as VERB-FINAL ___ed and the 5 ESSES. This textbook is also designed to help students increase their vocabularies.

Clear, well-organized speech minimizes confusion. Speaking clearly is also an unequivocal signal to others that the speaker is educated. Speaking concisely also indicates a high level of literacy. And rightly so.

IF YOU WISH TO WRITE WELL YOU MUST SPEAK WELL.
The two skills are "Siamese twins." They cannot be separated.

One can learn to read English, or any other language, with a low level of speaking skills. But unless one speaks English well, one cannot understand the finer points of meaning.

ENGLISH PRONUNCIATION, MEANING & SPELLING THREE EXAMPLES

1. Very few words in English are pronounced the way they are spelled. A famous example is the word "read." An irregular verb, "read" is spelled exactly the same in the present and past tenses. But the pronunciations are different.
   a. In the PRESENT TENSE "read" is pronounced /rid/, as in neat, clean, dream, real. The vowel sound for ALPHABET LETTERS ea is the front high tense, "long" sound /i/.
   b. But in the PAST TENSE "read" is pronounced /rɛd/, as in the color red. The vowel sound is mid-front, short /ɛ/, as in bread, head, lead.

Obviously the English alphabet is not very phonemic. That means that only a few English alphabet letters carry a single sound. They are d l m n p r & f (except, of course, the preposition of).

Most alphabet consonant letters, especially those that combine with ALPHABET LETTER h (ch gh ph th) represent 2, 3, and even 4 different phonemes or sounds!

2. The 5 ALPHABET VOWEL LETTERS a e i o u are even more flexible. They overlap and share 13 very different vowel sounds. Add the 3 diphthongs /ai/, /au/ & /ɔi/ and you have a total of

16 VOWEL PHONEMES or DISTINCTIVE SOUNDS.

3. Another interesting feature of the ENGLISH ALPHABET is the case of ALPHABET LETTERS w and y. Both are CONSONANTS at the beginnings and in middles of words, mostly when followed by a vowel sound. For example.

went, wave, bówer, cóward & young, yell, lawyer, toying,

   a. At WORD-ENDINGS, however, ALPHABET LETTER w is really an extension of the VOWEL SOUND that precedes it. For example.

   flew (/u/) blow (/o/) claw (/ɔ/).

   b. ALPHABET LETTER y, however, usually sounds like /i/ at the ends of words. For example.

   baby, ready, honey, funny.

THE INTERNATIONAL PHONETIC ALPHABET

The phoneme diacritics or characteristic sound symbols in this text derive from THE INTERNATIONAL PHONETIC ALPHABET (IPA).

BACKGROUND:

THE INTERNATIONAL PHONETIC ALPHABET (IPA) was put together about one hundred years ago by Paul Passy and his colleagues who together founded the Phonetic Teacher's Association.

They chose symbols to represent sounds in all the world's 3,000-plus languages. Nearly all of these symbols come from FRENCH, GERMAN, the SLAVIC languages and ENGLISH.

THE INTERNATIONAL PHONETIC ALPHABET (IPA) symbols were really intended to be characteristic sounds or PHONEMES. They were NOT intended to represent ALLOPHONES or phonetic variations, the many ways a single sound can be pronounced. A more appropriate title for the IPA would be THE INTERNATIONAL PHONEMIC ALPHABET.[1]

NOTE: The phoneme symbols in this text represent the characteristic sounds of the American English dialect called Standard American English. Standard American English is the variety spoken by most well-educated native speakers of American English, and by radio and television commentators.

1. MacMahon, M.K.C. 1995. The International Phonetic Alphabet. In Kirsten Malmkjaer, ed. THE LINGUISTICS ENCYCLOPEDIA. NY, Routledge: 219–224.

HOW PHONEMES (SOUNDS) ARE PRODUCED

All phonemes are produced by two interactive physiological processes. They are:

1. POINT OF ARTICULATION, the places in the mouth and throat where a sound is created, and
2. MANNER OF ARTICULATION, or the many ways the parts of the mouth shape the air as it rises from the lungs. FOR EXAMPLE:

Point of Articulation

The phonemes /t/ and /d/ are PLOSIVE STOPS. That means you bounce the tip of the tongue off the alveolar ridge (the roots of the upper teeth).

Manner of Articulation

At the same time you explode the air coming up from the throat.

NOTE: Each phoneme symbol in this text has a single value, just like numbers.

THE AMERICAN ENGLISH PHONEMES IN THIS TEXT

Several of the phoneme symbols in this text differ from symbols in the INTERNATIONAL PHONETIC ALPHABET (IPA). This is because American English sounds are distinctive. Many of the IPA symbols do not fit some English sounds very well.

Furthermore, English phoneme:spelling relationships are easier to learn when the symbols closely resemble English alphabet letters.

EXAMPLES:

5 CONSONANT SYMBOLS

TEXT	IPA	TEXT	IPA	TEXT	IPA	TEXT	IPA	TEXT	IPA
č	tʃ	ǰ	dʒ	y̲	j	š	ʃ	ž	ʒ
for chips		for jump		for yes		for ship		for garáge	

THE 3 DIPHTHONGS

TEXT	IPA	TEXT	IPA	TEXT	IPA
ai	aI	au	aU	⊐i	⊐I
kite		cow		toy	

American English Phonemes

THE 13 VOWEL PHONEMES

Most American English vowels are produced in the upper 2/3 of the mouth. To more easily visualize where each vowel is located, we divide the mouth into 3 horizontal and 3 vertical sections.

Figure 1. The 13 Vowel Phonemes.

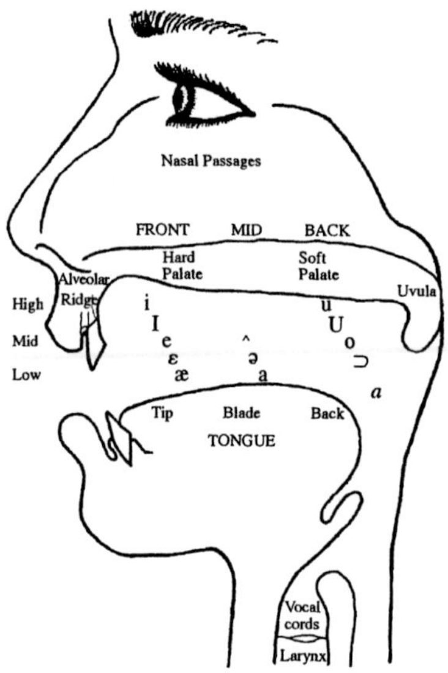

THE 3 DIPHTHONG PHONEMES

Each of the 3 American English diphthongs are combinations of 2 vowels.

1. MID LOW FRONT /a/ + HIGH FRONT /i/ = /ai/
2. MID LOW FRONT /a/ + HIGH BACK /u/ = /au/
3. MID LOW BACK /⊃/ + HIGH FRONT /i/ = /⊃i/

Figure 2. The 3 Diphthong Phonemes.

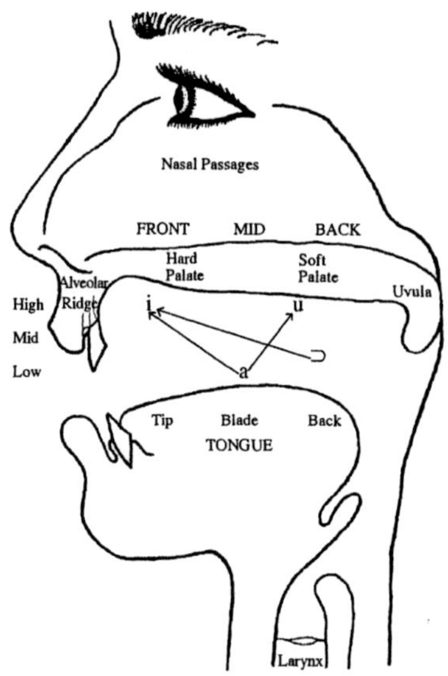

The 25 Consonant Phonemes

There are 6 traditional consonant phoneme groups. The rationale is based on how the tongue, back-of-the-mouth, throat and larynx (glottis) shape the air coming up from the lungs.

Figure 3. 7 Plosive Stops.

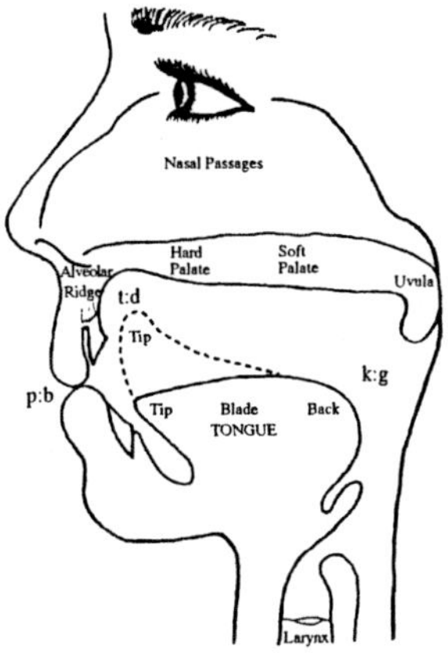

Figure 4. 9 Fricatives.

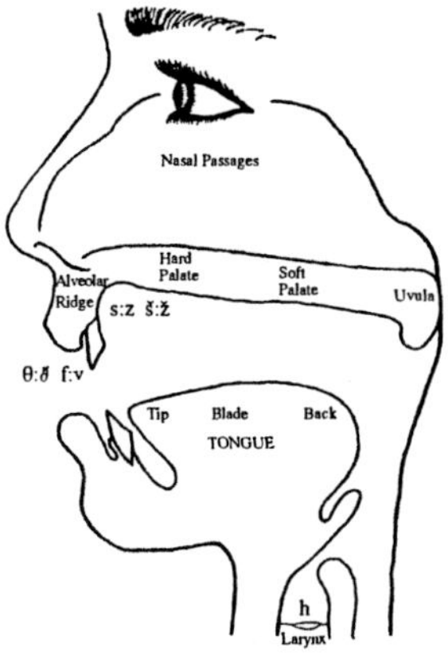

Figure 5. 3 Nasals.

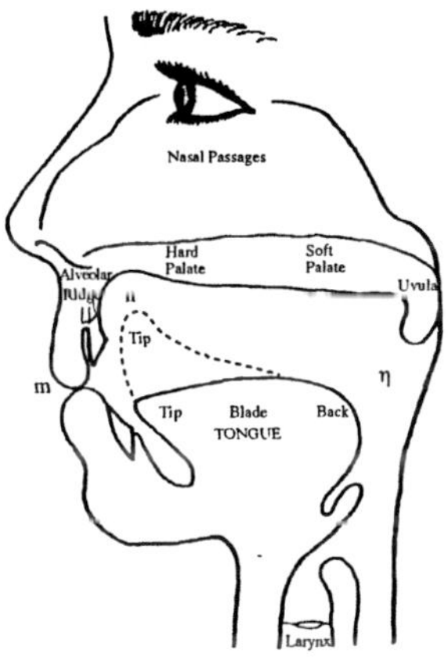

Figure 6. 2 Affricates.

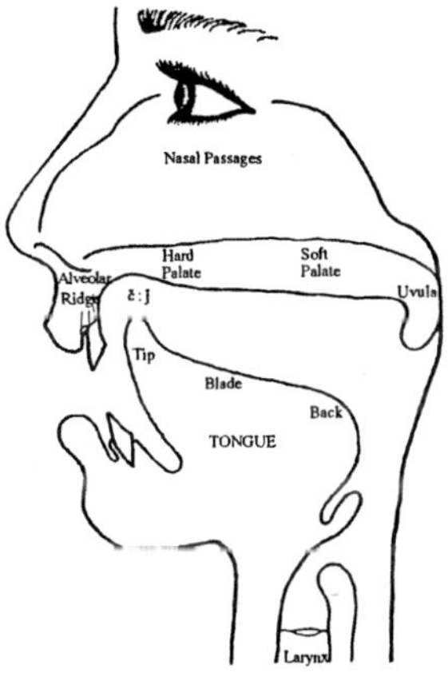

Figure 7. 2 Liquids.

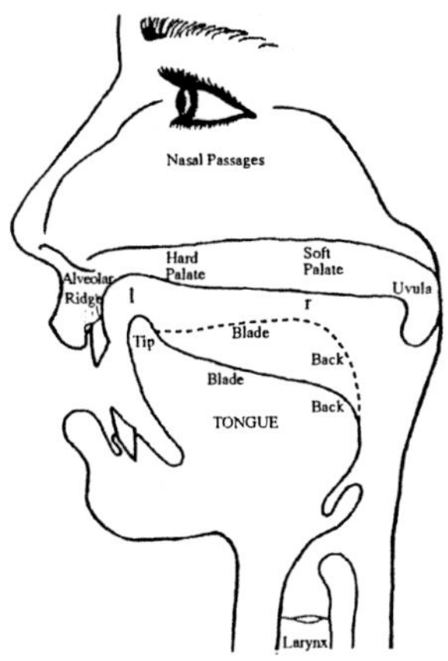

Figure 8. 2 Glides.

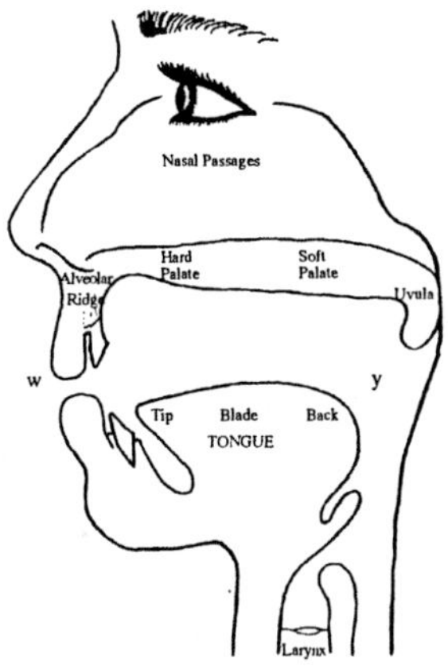

Analyzing English phonemes according to how the air is modified is not very helpful when students wish to practice pronouncing English sounds.

In many other languages and even in some English dialects, most vowels, consonants and diphthongs are created in the lower 1/2 of the mouth. That means the tongue remains low in the mouth.

Most Standard American English sounds, however, are produced in the upper 2/3 of the mouth. The tongue remains high in the mouth most of the time.

Figure 9. The 25 American English Consonant Phonemes.

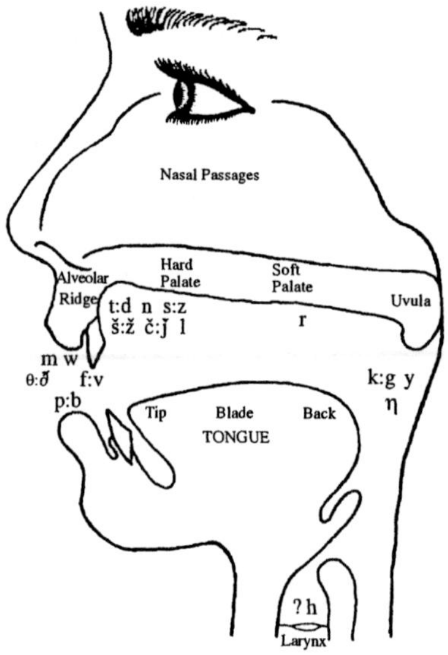

To reflect the physical realities of American English, the consonants in Chapter III are divided into

6 CONSONANT PHONEME CATEGORIES

1. APICO-ALVEOLARS 2. INTERDENTALS 3. LABIO-DENTALS
4. BI-LABIALS 5. PALATO-VELARS 6. GLOTTALS.

1. The 10 apico-alveolar/upper teeth root ridge consonants:

2 stops	1 nasal	1 liquid	4 fricatives	2 affricates
t & d	n	l	s & z š & ž	č & ǰ

2. The 2 interdental fricatives/tongue-between-the-teeth consonants: θ & ð
3. The 2 labio-dental fricatives/upper teeth & lower lip consonants: f & v
4. The 4 bi-labial/both lips consonants:

2 stops	1 nasal	1 glide
p & b	m	w

5. The 5 palato-velar/back-of-the-mouth consonants:

2 stops	1 liquid	1 nasal	1 glide
k & g	r	η	y

6. THE 2 glottal/vocal cords consonants:

1 stop	1 fricative
?	h

LANGUAGES OTHER THAN ENGLISH

Because the consonants in many languages are pronounced in the lower 1/2 of the mouth, the tongue remains low most of the time.

Figure 10. A Sample of Non-English Consonant Phonemes.

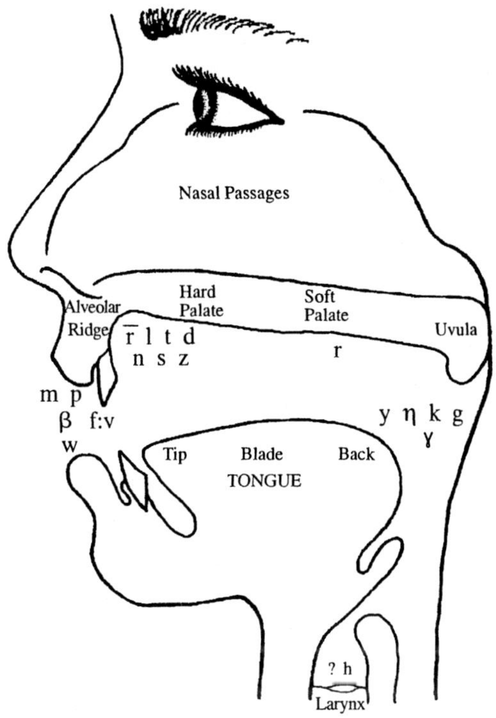

Three Pronunciation Differences Between Standard American English and Other Languages.

1. In many languages consonants, such as ALPHABET LETTERS r & l are usually produced towards the back of the mouth where the back of the tongue closes off the air coming up from the throat. This is one reason why American English /r/ is hard to pronounce.

   In Haitian Kreyol and French, English /r/ is a "squeezed" sound, the fricative /ɣ/.

   In Spanish, German and the Slavic languages /r/ is produced by rolling the tongue against the upper teeth ridge, as /r̄/.

   Languages, such as Chinese, Korean and Japanese do not have English /r/, especially at the beginnings of words. A kind of /r/ is produced at the end of the syllable /ʔər/.

   Chinese, Korean and Japanese /l/, however, is pronounced half-way between English /l/ and English /r/.

2. The 6 consonants m p b w f v are pronounced differently in languages other than English.

   In Spanish, German and the Slavic languages, and in many Indic (India) languages m p b w f v are often combined into a single sound: the bi-labial fricative /β/. One of the few times you can hear some differences between m p b w f v in these languages is at the beginnings of words.

Furthermore, in Spanish, German, the Slavic languages and in many Indic languages m p b w f v are articulated without the puffs of air they have to have when one is speaking English.

3. The 2 English affricates /č/ & /ǰ/ combine a plosive stop with a fricative (squeezing the air). Both are bounced off the alveolar ridge. In many other languages /č/ & /ǰ/ are pronounced lower down, against the bottom edges of the upper teeth.

   The IPA symbols /tʃ/ & /dʒ/ are commonly articulated as though they were the fricatives /š/ & /ž/.

Figure 11. The 2 "Affricates" in Other Languages.

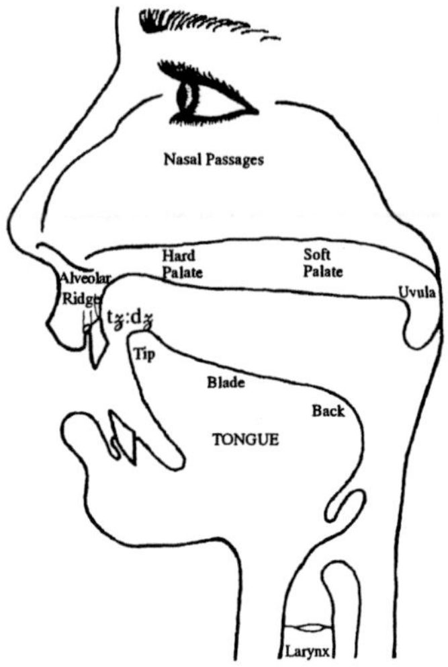

Figure 12. The 2 Affricates in English.

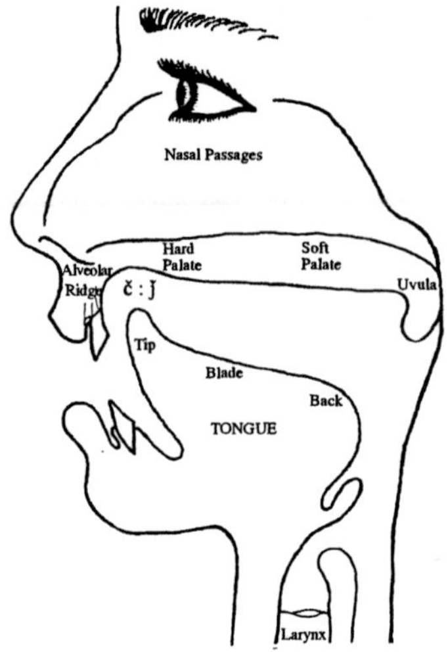

4. The number of vowels is often 1/2 that in English: 8.
5. This is because each non-English vowel combines 2 separate English vowels.

Figure 13. Vowel Phonemes in Some Other Languages.

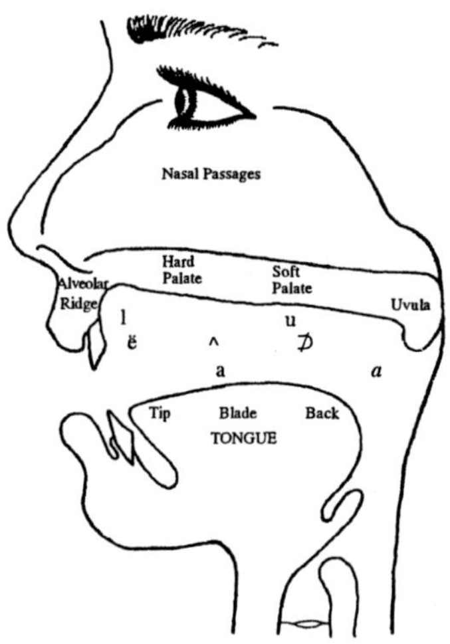

EXAMPLES:

Non-English	English	Non-English	English
/ı/	/i/ : /I/	/ĕ/	/e/ : /ɛ/
/a/ : /ɑ/	/æ/ : /a/ : /ɑ/	/u/	/u/ : /U/
/ɒ/	/O/ : /ɔ/	/Λ/	/ə/

SUPRASEGMENTALS

Just learning to pronounce the sounds of Standard American English reasonably well is not enough. Although correct pronunciation is essential to effective communication, one must learn to "sing."

Every language has its unique "symphonic" combination of "singing." They are the SUPRASEGMENTALS, the elements of speech that accompany articulation.

As in all languages, AMERICAN ENGLISH SUPRASEGMENTALS consist of many elements that work together simultaneously. 8 of the most important are

1. VOICE QUALITY
2. SPEED
3. SYLLABLE STRESS
4. PHRASE ACCENT
5. PAUSE
6. RHYTHM/SYNCOPATION
7. MAINTAINING RISE
8. RISE-FALL

Together these elements create INTONATION CONTOUR, the melodic line of words, phrases and sentences. SUPRASEGMENTALS make speaking in every language pleasanter and more comprehensible. Here are 2 examples.

EXAMPLE 1:

We lóve chócolate cáke.

a. Every word in this statement has its own rhythm and length. Note the slight pause between the two phrases.

PHRASE #1		PHRASE #2	
			cá
	lóve		k
		chócolate	e
We			.

b. Whenever you see a stress symbol/accent mark over a vowel in a syllable as in

   a. PHRASE #1 "lóve"

   b. PHRASE #2 "chócolate" and "cake,"

RAISE THE PITCH OF YOUR VOICE. "SING" UP

c. Because "cáke" is more important in meaning here than "chócolate," the word "cáke" rises higher in pitch. If, however, the speaker wishes to make "chocolate" more important meaning-wise, then "chocolate" is pitched higher than "cake."

PHRASE #1 PHRASE #2

chó
lóve co
late
We cá
k
e

EXAMPLE 2:

Schóol is ópen todáy.

PHRASE #1 PHRASE #2

ó
pen
School is tod
á
y
.

NOTE: Because "ópen" is a QUALIFIER (much, most, yet, soon), its pitch level is usually higher than any other word in the sentence.

Text Format

SPEAKING AMERICAN ENGLISH WELL contains

1. A detailed Table of Contents
2. A List of Figures
3. A List of Tables
4. The Preface
5. 4 Chapters
   Chapter I: How to Use This Textbook
   Chapter II: The 13 Vowel Phonemes and the 3 Diphthongs
      a. Pronunciation and Review Exercises
      b. Doggerels, Limericks, Rhymes, Riddles and Songs
      c. Dialogues and Trialogues
   Chapter III: The 25 Consonant Phonemes
      a. Pronunciation and Review Exercises
      b. Doggerels, Limericks, Rhymes, Riddles and Songs
      c. Dialogues and Trialogues

Chapter IV: American English Suprasegmentals Or How To "Sing" in American English.
   a. The 8 Most Common Suprasegmental Elements
   b. 4 Common Sentence Contours for Statements and Questions
   c. The Complex Verb Tenses

6. Appendix I: A List of Nearly 100 Song Titles

AN OVERVIEW OF CHAPTERS II, III & IV

Chapter II: Vowel Phonemes & Chapter III: Consonant Phonemes

Both chapters contain a variety of exercises to accommodate all skill levels.

Beginners can work through the drills and practice pronunciation further using the doggerels, limericks, rhymes, riddles and songs and the review exercises.

As students improve, they will benefit from the graded dialogues of Levels I, I/II and II/III. Each is designed to help students practice sound combinations in a conversation-like format.

Syllable stress and phrase accent are marked virtually everywhere. Most of the exercises are spaced to show English phrasing.

There is also a series of GRAMMAR-RELATED pronunciation sections, such as WORD-FINAL ___ED in Chapter III, page 92, and THE 5 ___ESSES in Chapter III, pages 103–108.

AUDIOTAPES

All of the exercises in this text are on the audiotapes.

DRILLS, DOGGERELS, RHYMES, RIDDLES, SONGS and DIALOGUES, are repeated twice.

The first repetition of a particular exercise or line separates it into phrases and is spoken very slowly. Articulation and phrasing are exaggerated.

The second repetition is sentence-long, slightly faster, and closer to normal speech.

USE OF THE AUDIO TAPES IS RECOMMENDED.

FOUR TECHNIQUES

Be as precise as you can when articulating a sound, a syllable, a word and/or phrase. Practice each exercise over and over systematically.

FIRST: SLOW DOWN. It is easier to learn a difficult set of sounds when you take your time.

SECOND: Be sure to "sing" what you are practicing. Incorporate suprasegmentals, such as syllable stress, pause and rise-fall whenever you can.

THIRD: And most important: EXAGGERATE! Overdo the pronunciations and suprasegmentals for as long as necessary. It takes a lot of practice to become comfortable speaking another language.

FOURTH: Be sure to pause between phrases and between vowel:consonant blends. Small pauses between words and phrases are necessary for at least two equally important reasons.

1. Small pauses enable the listener to easily understand what the speaker is saying.
2. They help you articulate difficult sound combinations more easily.

Two More Suggestions

1. Study Figure 14. Become familiar with the inside of your mouth and throat. Use a mirror to help you identify different locations in the mouth and throat.
2. Write in the phonemes for as many of the exercises as possible.

Figure 14. The Human Vocal Apparatus: Mouth, Nasals and Throat Segments.

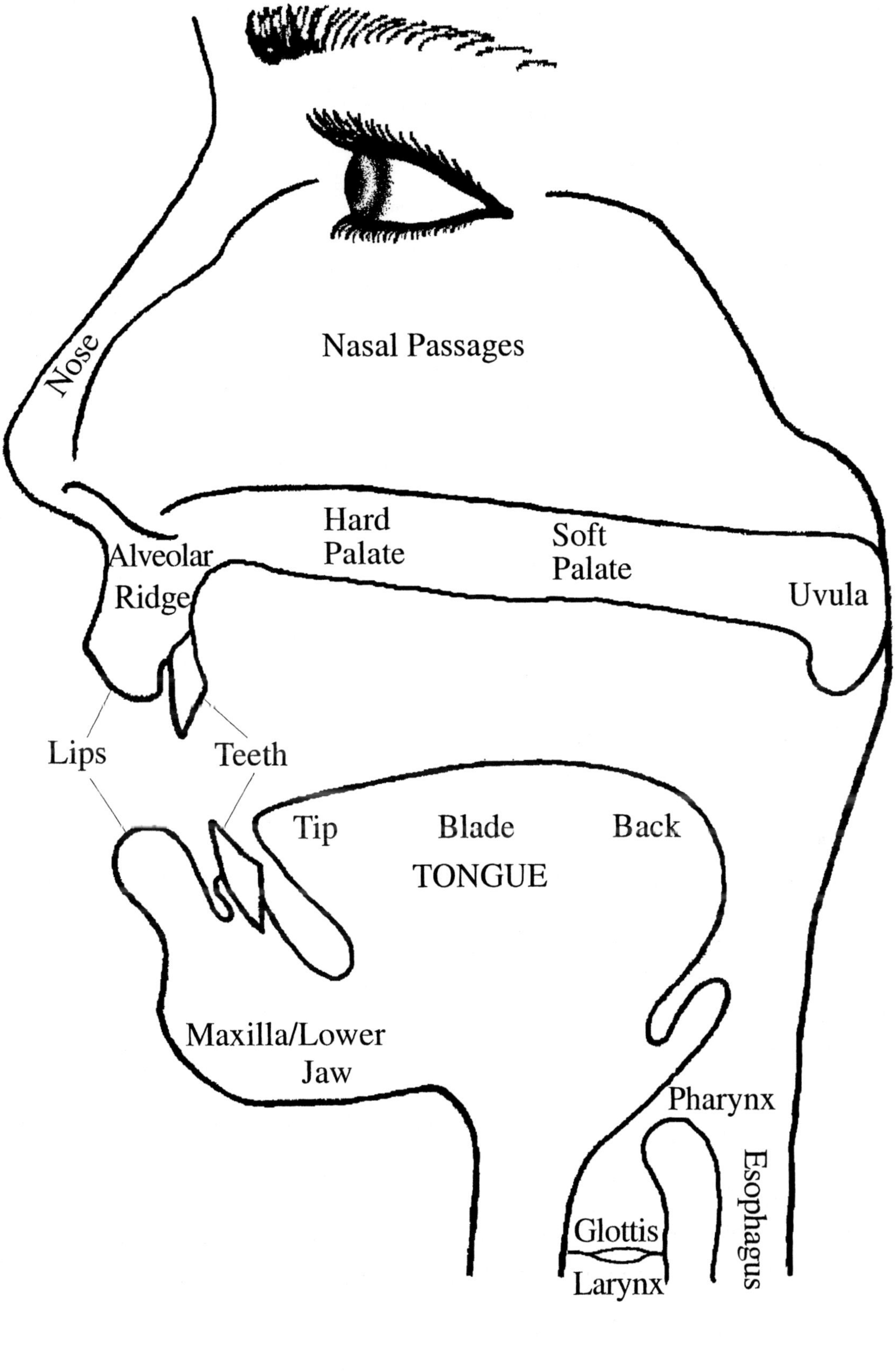

Table 1. American English Vowel Phonemes. The 13 Vowel Phonemes and the 3 Diphthongs.

PHONEMES	POINT OF ARTICULATION	SAMPLE WORDS
/i/	tense high front vowel	read, beet, concéive, swéetie, báby
/I/	lax mid-high front vowel	bit, limb, myth, women, lítter, ínto
/e/	tense mid-front vowel	late, wait, say mélee, weigh, áble
/ɛ/	lax mid-low front vowel	let, said, says, corréct, friend
/æ/	tense low front vowel	cap, lamp, hand, at, and, cándle
/a/	lax low mid vowel	cop, cot, pótter, onto, cómplex
/ɑ/	lax low back vowel	car, want, wash, fáther, heart, calm
/ʌ/	lax mid-central vowel	cup, putt, love, cómfort, enóugh
/ə/	extra-lax mid-low central vowel (in UNSTRESSED SYLLABLES ONLY)	aróund, abóut, anóther, a, Clára
/u/	tense high back vowel	boot, food, to/too/two, flute, new
/U/	lax high-mid back vowel	could/would/should, bush, cook, put
/o/	tense mid back vowel	note, wrote, toe, coat, bow, though
/ɔ/	tense mid-low back vowel	caught, four/for/fore, thought, mall

NOTE: A "tense" vowel is muscularly tight and therefore, takes longer to pronounce than a "lax" or more relaxed vowel.

THE 3 DIPHTHONGS

PHONEMES	POINT OF ARTICULATION	SAMPLE WORDS
/ai/	low front to front high vowels	bite, time, night, sigh, fly, climb
/au/	low front to back high vowels	cow, bow, mouth, sound, astóund
/ɔi/	mid-back to front high vowels	toy, boy, annóy, soy, joy, Floyd

SYLLABIC /əl/

PHONEMES	POINT OF ARTICULATION	SAMPLE WORDS
/əl/	extra-short mid-low central vowel + LIQUID /l/ (in UNSTRESSED SYLLABLES ONLY)	búbble, lábel, táble, búndle allówance, alléviate, alláy

SYLLABIC /Ur/

PHONEMES	POINT OF ARTICULATION	SAMPLE WORDS
/Ur/	mid-high back /U/ + LIQUID /r/	bútter, earn, fern, girl, múrder

SYLLABIC /er/

PHONEMES	POINT OF ARTICULATION	SAMPLE WORDS
/er/	long mid front vowel	bare/bear/bear, hair, heir, Máry

NOTE: The Liquids /l/ & /r/ are the only phonemes that shape the air in the mouth by curling the tongue. All the other vowels, diphthongs and consonants shape the air by exploding, squeezing, or pushing it out of the nose.

ALL AMERICAN ENGLISH VOWELS AND DIPHTHONGS ARE VOICED

Table 2. American English Consonant Phonemes. The 25 Phonemes and /hw/.

PHONEMES	POINT OF ARTICULATION	SAMPLE WORDS
/t/	voiceless apico-alveolar stop	top, pot, two/too/to, mátter
/d/	voiced apico-alveolar stop	dot, don't, mud, múddle, fried
/p/	voiceless bilabial stop	pot, pan, ópen, appárent, flop
/b/	voiced bilabial stop	belíeve, abóut, róbber, stab
/k/	voiceless palato-velar stop	keep, skin, make, tack, pick, ink
/g/	voiced palato-vela stop	girl, got, bígger, agáin, bring
/ʔ/	voiced glottal stop	anóther, émpty, an, and, únder
/s/	voiceless apico-alveolar fricative	sun/son, mássive, class, amíss
/z/	voiced apico-alveolar fricative	zípper, crázy, hands, babies
/š/	voiceless apico-alveolar fricative	show, Sean, míssion, crash
/ž/	voiced apico-alveolar fricative	Jácques, méasure, garáge
/θ/	voiceless inter-dental fricative	think, thumb, cloth, mouth
/ð/	voiced inter-dental fricative	this/these, clothe, mouthe
/f/	voiced labio-dental fricative	fun, few, áfter, efféct, stuff
/v/	voiceless labio-dental fricative	véry, éver, óven, stove, move
/h/	voiceless glottal fricative	hat, house, how, héaven, ahéad
/č/	voiceless apico-dental affricate	chips, mátches, much, bunch
/ǰ/	voiced apico-dental affricate	judge, géntle, fudge, stíngy
/n/	voiced apico-dental nasal	not, númber, fúnny, men, depénd
/m/	voiced bilabial nasal	móther, númber, clams, stamp
/ŋ/	voiced palato-velar nasal	sing, sang, sung, song, wing
/l/	voiced alveolar liquid	love, flówer, sílly, bell, all
/r/	voiced palatal liquid	run, barn, fúrnace, fárther
/w/	voiced bilabial glide	want, twin, swim, tówer, láwyer
/y/	voiced palato-velar glide	yes, yéllow, tíre, tile, flyer
/hw/	voiceless glottal bilabial fricative	when, where, what, why, whíle

CHAPTER II

The 13 Vowel Phonemes and the 3 Diphthongs

INTRODUCTION

To gain the greatest benefit from this textbook, students should practice articulating the exercises aloud as much as possible.

Whenever possible write in the phonemes.

Doing both will maximize one's ability to recognize relationships between the sounds and how words are spelled.

One's proficiency in pronouncing new words correctly will improve.

The accompanying tapes should help.

SYLLABLE STRESS & PHRASE ACCENT

Most of the WORDS in the exercises, SINGLE-SYLLABLE and MULTI-SYLLABLE, carry an ACCENT MARK over a vowel. This is done to sensitize the student to

1. identify the STRESSED SYLLABLE in MULTI-SYLLABLE words, and at the same time,
2. recognize when to raise the PITCH of one's voice in a PHRASE (PHRASE ACCENT).

FOR EXAMPLE:

Jím, cléan the kítchen sínk.

ANALYSIS:

1. The sentence above consists of 3 distinct phrases:
   a. Jím
   b. cléan
   c. the kítchen sínk.
2. 4 of the 5 words in the sentence carry an accent mark over the vowel.
3. All 4 words signal a rise in voice level or pitch
4. Only two-syllable "kítchen" identifies both
   a. kítchen's stressed syllable, and
   b. kítchen's accent or pitch rise, as in the phrase ". . . the kítchen sínk."

REMEMBER: WORK SYSTEMATICALLY.

1. SOUND OUT EVERY SOUND.
2. SOUND OUT EVERY SYLLABLE.
3. RAISE THE PITCH OF YOUR VOICE ON THE STRESSED SYLLABLES.
4. LINK WORDS INTO PHRASES USING THE ELEMENTS OF INTONATION CONTOUR (CHAPTER IV: SUPRASEGMENTALS)
5. LINK PHRASES INTO SENTENCES. AND MOST OF ALL

"SING" THE EXERCISES AS YOU SPEAK.

Figure 15. The 13 Vowel Phonemes.

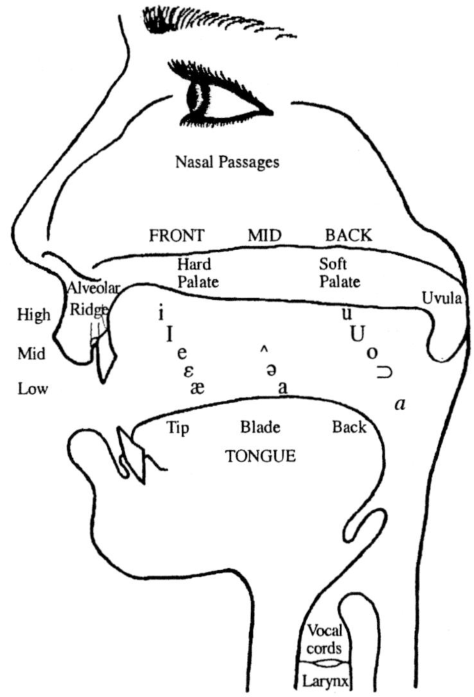

Table 3. Sample Words—Vowel Phonemes.

PHONEME	SAMPLE WORDS	PHONEME	SAMPLE WORDS
/i/	read, beet, belíeve, báby meat/meet/mete, sweetie precéde, knead, redéem	/u/	food, cool, to/too/two, lose flew/flue/flu, new/gnu fruit, due/do/dew, dual/duel
/I/	bit, limb, ínto, myth, wómen different, insíst, wínter drípless, hídden, sieve, guilt	/U/	cook, could/would/should, full put, kapút, wood, stood bush, cúrtain, burst, worse
/e/	wait, take, say, weigh, áble freight, break, stale, heir mail/male, vary/Mary/hairy	/o/	boat, note, bow, toe, though stone, float, vócal, comb drole, close/close, broke
/ɛ/	wet, said, says, friend bread, temple, tréasure héavensent, Septémber	/ɔ/	caught, thought, for/four/fore door, floor, dog, hálter, sore chalk, law, wáter, maráud
/æ/	man, hándle, lamp, at, and hábit, plan, párity, tángy standard, apparátus, ánger	/ʌ/	cup, love, enóugh, sun/son flood, hush, gun, gulf, trough cóurage, cóver, wórry, húnger
/a/	cop, pótter, ónto, cómplex módern, fóllow, dócument voluntéer, knock, bóttle	/ə/	agáin, anóther, abóut, Clára allów, voluntéer, amóunt, a amóng, amóral, occúr, alóne
/*a*/	wash, want, bar, heart, calm fáther, róbber, bóther, tar dódge, cárpet, sórry, odd		

/i/ is a long, tense vowel. /I/ is a shorter, more relaxed vowel.

TO ARTICULATE /i/, smile brightly and keep your tongue high.

1. Pull the back and middle of the tongue up against the soft palate (the back of the mouth).
2. Flatten the tongue and press the sides of the tongue hard against the insides of the upper molars (the back teeth).
3. The tip of the tongue is high on the alveolar ridge (the roots of the upper teeth), but doesn't touch them.

Figure 16.

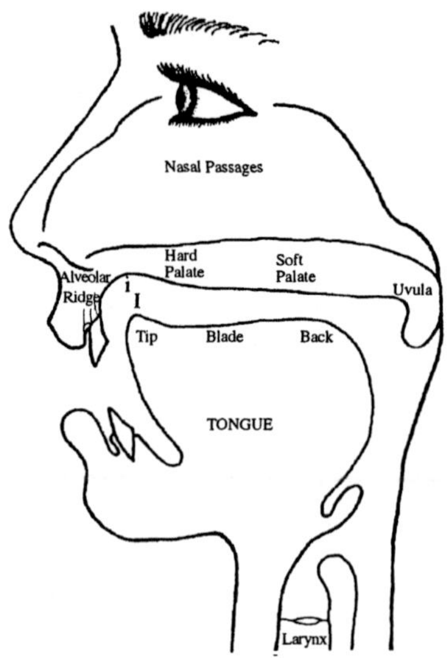

TO ARTICULATE /I/, relax your jaw, but keep pressing the sides of your tongue against the insides of the upper molars.

SPEAKING & PHONEME WRITING CONTRAST EXERCISES: /i/ & /I/

long, tense /i/	short, relaxed /I/
1. Béat the héat.	1. A bít of spít.
2. Sée the bée.	2. Ín a mínute.
3. Pléase be a swéetie.	3. Sit stíll untíl I fínish.
4. Déal me thrée, báby.	4. Quíck! The kítten is síck.

PHONEME:SPELLING COMBINATIONS

Long /i/ has a variety of spellings: éa as in Béat, ée as in sée, ie as in swéetie, and end-of-a-word ALPHABET LETTER y as in baby. So does short /I/: lísten, confusion, áction, Rússian.

NOTE: To correctly pronounce DEFINITE ARTICLE the, see Chapter III, page 137. For INDEFINITE ARTICLE a/an, see Chapter II, page 51. qu is nearly always pronounced /kw/: quick /kwIk/, quíet /kwáyIt/.

FIND /i/ & /I/ IN THESE LIMERICKS

AN /i/ LIMERICK

There wás a swéet lády from Níce

Who decíded to jóin the políce.

She chéats the drúg déalers

Who deal spéed to pre-téeners

And héaves them úpstate to Síng-Sing.

VOCABULARY		
Níce	/nis/	is a French city on the Mediterranean. In English the adjective nice is pronounced /nais/.
er		See Chapter III, pages 132–134 for er, SYLLABIC /Ur/.
heaves	/hivz/	Throwing something heavy.

AN /I/ LIMERICK

In a pít sits thín Míster Stíkk,

Who suppórts his kíds with a píck,

Which he swíngs dáy and níght

In the ábsence of líght

Coming úp ónce a mónth for a flíck.

THE LIMERICK /lÍmrIk/ is a form of humorous verse. It is said to have originated in Limerick, Ireland. Limerick poems first appeared in print in 1719 in Elizabeth Goose's SONGS FOR THE NURSERY, OR MOTHER GOOSE MELODIES FOR CHILDREN. This book was originally published by Boston printer Thomas Fleet, Elizabeth Goose's husband. In 1846 Edward Lear published a book titled A BOOK OF NONSENSE, a collection of his own and other people's limericks.

NOTE: Both reader and writer take advantage of POETIC LICENSE. That means we can adjust a word's usual pronunciations, rhythms and syllable stresses to fit the rhyming pattern.
ng See Chapter III pages 169–173 for ng, agna /ŋ/.

FIND /i/ & /I/ IN THIS RHYME

Néedles and pins, néedles and pins.

When a wóman márries, her tróubles begín.

FIND /i/ & /I/ IN THIS DOGGEREL

Once I fóund an ápple pip and stúck it in the gróund.

And when I cáme to lóok at it a tíny shoot I fóund.

The shóot grew úp and úp each dáy, it sóon becáme a trée.

I pícked the rósy ápples then, and áte them for my téa.

VOCABULARY

pip	/pIp/	An apple seed.
shoot	/šut/	A tiny plant.

FIND /I/ IN THIS DOGGEREL

Héy, díddle díddle, the cát and the fíddle,

The ców jumped óver the móon.

The líttle dog láughed to sée such spórt,

And the dísh ran awáy with the spóon.

VOCABULARY

fíddle	/fÍdəl/	Another name for a violin.
sport	/sp⊃rt/	Fun and games.

FIND /i/ IN THIS DOGGEREL

Sée, sée! Whát do I sée?

A hórse's head where its táil should be.

FIND /i/ & /I/ IN THIS RHYME

Thrée yóung wómen in a téeny wíckiup,

Squéezed ínto a setée,

Drínking tea from chína cúps.

In spíte of the límits of spáce and mótion,

They dwélt in accórd, eschéwing commótion.

VOCABULARY

wíckiup	/wÍkiyΛp/	A round Apache (Native American) house.
setée	/sɛtí/	A small sofa, also called a love seat.
dwélt in accórd	/dwɛl tInək⊃rd/	Lived together peacefully.
eschéwing	/?ɛšuwiη/	Giving up.
commótion	/kəmóšIn/	A lot of fuss, noise and trouble.

FIND /i/ & /I/ IN THIS DOGGEREL

Thrée little kíttens lóst their míttens,

Só they begán to cry.

"Oh, móther dear, we sádly fear

That wé have lóst our míttens."

"You bád little kíttens!

You've lóst your míttens!

Nów you shall háve no píe!"

LEVEL I: AN /i/ & /I/ DIALOGUE: CLEAN THE SINK

Tim: Jím, cléan the kítchen sínk.

Jim: Cléan it yoursélf, Tim.

Tim: I cléaned it yésterday.

Jim: I cléaned it yésterday, tóo.

Tim: Nó you dídn't!

Jim: Yés I díd!

Tim: Wáit a mínute. Máybe we bóth cléaned the sínk.

Jim: I thínk yóu're ríght.

Tim: Then let's bóth cléan the sínk évery dáy.

Jim: It will kéep us from árguing abóut it.

Tim: Is it a déal?

Jim: It's a déal.

FIND /i/ & /I/ IN THIS DIALOGUE

LEVEL II/III: AN /i/ & /I/ DIALOGUE: SWEETPEA AND THE SICK KITTEN

Sweetpea: Ílsa! Get óver here!

Ilsa: What ís it, Swéetpea?

Sweatpea: This kítten. It's límp.

Ilsa: Gée whíz! I thínk it's síck.

Sweetpea: It néeds to éat. Háve we any mílk in the frídge?

Ilsa: Féel its chést. Its bréathing seems amíss.

Sweetpea: It will pérish if we dón't táke it to a vét.

Ilsa: Wráp this bít of quílt aróund it.

Sweetpea: Gíve it a síp of mílk fírst.

Ilsa: Oh lóok! It's pérking úp. The mílk's doing the tríck.

VOCABULARY

frídge	/frIǰ/	Short for refrigerator, /rIfrÍǰUretUr/.
seems amíss	/símzəmÍs/	An elegant synonym for something's wrong.
vét	/vɛt/	Short for veterinarian, /vɛtUrInériyIn/ An animal doctor.
a bít of quílt	/?ə bÍt əvkwÍlt/	A piece of a blanket.
pérking úp	/pUrkiŋʌp/	Becoming more lively.
dóing the tríck	/dúwiŋ ðə trÍk/	An ídiom meaning the action is working.
an ídiom	/?ænÍdiyəm/	A phrase that has a single meaning.

See Chapter III, pages 181–186 for the glottal stop /?/.

VOWEL PHONEME:SPELLING REVIEW

/i/ & /I/

FILL IN THE SPACES UNDER THE ALPHABET LETTERS WITH WORDS FROM THE EXERCISES AND THEIR PHONEMES.

PHONEMES:		/i/		/I/
ALPHABET LETTERS:	ee	ea	eCe	i
AL:	bee see gee	beat heat cheat	precéde	bit sit spit
PH:				
AL:	sweet, three	please, deal, clean	recéde	mínute untíl
PH:				
AL:				
PH:				
AL:				
PH:				
AL:				
PH:				
AL:				
PH:				
AL:				
PH:				
AL:				
PH:				
AL:				
PH:				

eCe ALPHABET LETTER e is often followed by an ALPHABET CONSONANT (C) which is also followed by ALPHABET LETTER e. The SYLLABLE eCe is created and is usually pronounced /i/, as in secéde, stampéde, precéde, deléte.

THE 2 FRONT MID-HIGH VOWELS /e/ & /ɛ/ (Greek épsilon)

/e/ is a long, tense vowel /ɛ/ is a shorter, more relaxed vowel

/ɛ/ is slightly below and behind /e/, but more relaxed than /e/.

TO ARTICULATE /e/, smile.

1. Press the tongue against the soft palate.
2. At the same time drop the jaw a little.
3. Flatten the tongue and press the sides of the tongue against the insides of the upper molars (the back teeth).
4. NOTE: /e/ is pronounced using the same muscle group as /i/, but the tip & blade of the tongue are a tiny bit lower in the mouth.

Figure 17.

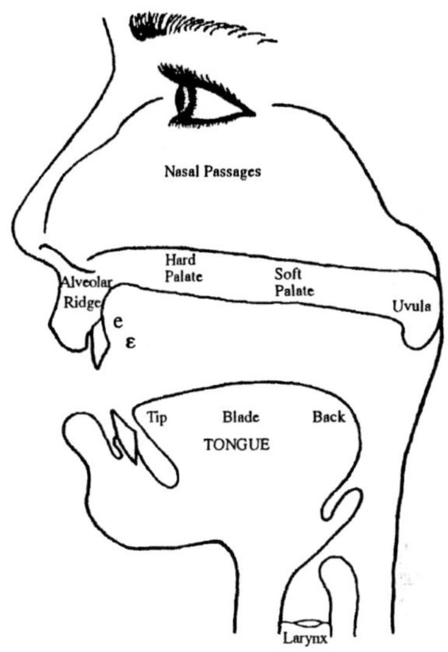

To articulate Greek épsilon /ɛ/, relax your smile and your tongue.

SPEAKING & PHONEME WRITING CONTRAST EXERCISES: /e/ & /ɛ/

long, tense /e/	short, relaxed /ɛ/
1. Héy, Wáyne. Wáit.	1. Bétter rest, Mel.
2. The pláte's on the táble.	2. Has Bétty réad the téxt?
3. Ábel is báking a cake.	3. Pénny is a wét hen.
4. Stáy and pláy with me, Fáye.	4. Lét the jéllo sét.

PHONEME:SPELLING COMBINATIONS

Long /e/ appears in at least 3 alphabet letter combinations. 1. ey as in Héy. See page 24 for the eCe spelling pattern. 2. ay as in Wayne, Fáye, play. 3. ate/able/Abel as in plate, table, Ábel. See page 30 for the aCe spelling pattern.

Short /ɛ/, Greek épsilon, has only 2 alphabet letter combinations: 1. e as in Betty, better, Mel, text, and 2. ea as in Past Tense read.

FIND /e/ & /ɛ/ IN THIS LIMERICK

A státely old lády named Gwén

Ran a bákeshop near Áttica pén.

She péddled áll of her cákes

To the trústy ínmates

Excépt those named Éd, Néd or Bén.

VOCABULARY

státely	/stétli/	Tall and elegant (classy).
bákeshop	/békšap/	Another word for bakery.
Attica	/ʔǽtIkə/	A prison in upstate New York.
pén	/pɛn/	A short form of penitentiary, or príson /prÍzIn/.
péddle	/pɛdəl/	To sell goods outdoors or from house-to-house.
trústy ínmates	/trΛsti yÍnmets/	Prisoners who do not try to escape.

FIND /ɛ/ IN THIS LIMERICK

Two génts who spent Lént in a tént,

Nearly drówned from a rént in one wáll.

Said the táller. "I'd cáll

My wife Ém and téll'er áll,

But I vówed abstinénce, so I cán't (kent)."

VOCABULARY

Lént	/lɛnt/	The Christian 40-day fast between Ash Wednesday & Easter Sunday.
rént	/rɛnt/	A tear or a rip in cloth.
Ém	/ʔɛm/	A woman's name, short for Emily or Emma.
ábstinence	/ʔǽbstInIns/	is the correct pronunciation. But abstinénce /ʔæbstInɛns/ fits the rhyme scheme. This change in stress is an example of poetic license. See page 19 for an explanation.

FIND /ɛ/ IN THIS RHYME

Góod, bétter, bést.

Néver rest

Till góod be bétter

And bétter, bést.

FIND /e/ & /ɛ/ IN THESE RIDDLES

QUESTION		ANSWER
Why is a chérry like a bóok?	BECAUSE	Bóth are réad (red).
Why is a hén like a pénny?	BECAUSE	Bóth have a héad and a táil.

FIND /e/ IN THIS DOGGEREL

Róck-a-bye báby on the tréetop.

When the wínd blèws the cr<u>ádle</u> will róck.

When the b<u>óugh</u> bréaks the crádle will fáll,

And dówn will come báby, bough, crádle and áll.

VOCABULARY

crádle	/krédəl/	A small, wooden rocking bed for a baby.
bough	/bo/ or /bau/	A thick tree branch.

LEVEL I/II: AN /e/ & /ɛ/ DIALOGUE: LABOR DAY

Ben: Septémber. My fávorite mónth.

Glenda: But Bén, súmmer vacátion is óver by Septémber.

Ben: Yes, Glénda, but remémber. Septémber means Lábor Day.

Glenda: Hmm. Lábor Day and the Lábor Day wéekend.

Ben: It's a gréat way to énd the súmmer.

Glenda: I guéss so. Stíll, I keep wíshing for a léngthier súmmer.

Ben: Only if you're wéalthy.

Glenda: Thén I would chíse the sún aróund the wórld.

Ben: Thát sounds like fún!

Glenda: I can dréam, can't I?

Ben: To máke your dréam come trúe, néxt time choose wéalthy párents.

Glenda: I'll attémpt to dó so the néxt time.

LEVEL II/III: AN /i/ & /e/ & /ɛ/ DIALOGUE: I NEED A VACATION!

Mamie: Jénnie, I néed a vacátion.

Jennie: Mé, too. An exténded rést.

Mamie: But vacátions are tóo expénsive!

Jennie: Máybe we can stáy hére.

Mamie: Gúests in our ówn néighborhood?

Jennie: Lét's preténd we're vacátioning on a désert ísland.

Mamie: Why nót! We'll stáy áll dáy at the béach.

Jennie: And bríng alóng some tásty fóods.

Mamie: And a gréat, bíg umbrélla!

Jennie: And a gréat, bíg blánket.

Mamie: Thís will bé a vacátion we'll réally enjóy.

Jennie: And a réally chéap one, tóo.

Mamie: Let's dó it!

VOWEL PHONEME:SPELLING REVIEW

/e/ & /ɛ/

FILL IN THE SPACES UNDER THE ALPHABET LETTERS WITH WORDS FROM THE EXERCISES AND THEIR PHONEMES.

PHONEMES:	/e/					/ɛ/	
ALPHABET LETTERS:	ey	ey	ai	ea	aCe	e	ea
AL:	lády báby	hey	wait	great	plate bake	better	wéalthy
PH:							
AL:	Wayne				státely	let	read
PH:							
AL:	stay				ínmate	Septémber	
PH:							
AL:					vacátion	jéllo	
PH:							
AL:							
PH:							
AL:							
PH:							
AL:							
PH:							
AL:							
PH:							
AL:							
PH:							

aCe — ALPHABET LETTER a is often followed by an ALPHABET CONSONANT (C) which is also followed by ALPHABET LETTER e, creating the SYLLABLE aCe. ALPHABET LETTER a is then pronounced /e/, as in wake, late, fame, race.

THE THREE FRONT, MID AND BACK LOW VOWELS: /æ/ & /a/ & /ɑ/

Figure 18. Front /æ/ is long & tense.

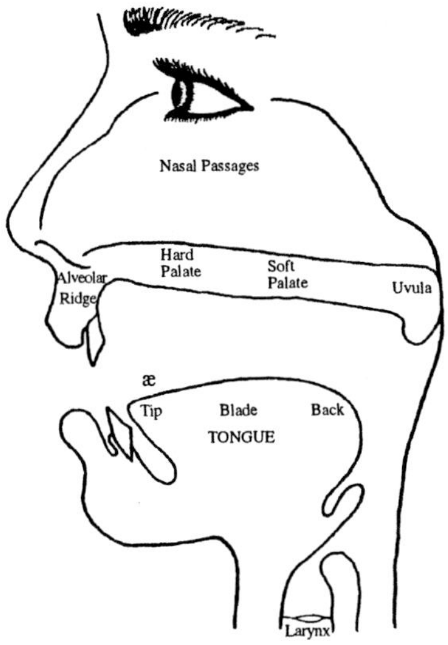

Figure 19. Mid /a/ & Back /ɑ/ are short & relaxed.

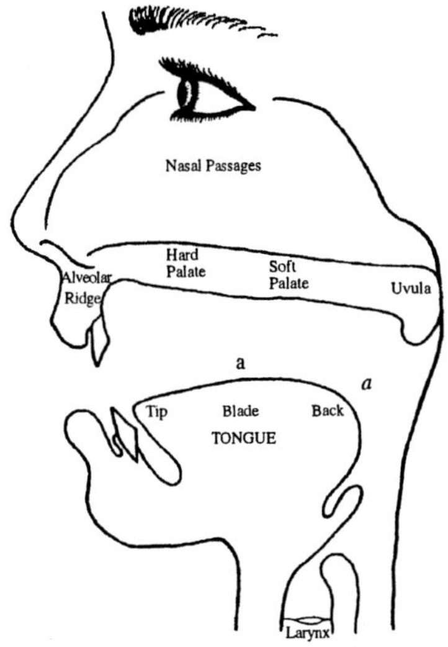

TO ARTICULATE LONG /æ/, smile!!!

1. Press the back of the tongue against the back of the mouth.
2. Then press the tongue's tip against the bottom teeth.

REMEMBER:

ALL LONG VOWELS LIKE /æ/ REQUIRE A LOT OF MUSCLE POWER!

SPEAKING & PHONEME WRITING EXERCISES: long, tense /æ/

1. Can Hárry cátch the cát?

2. I have a <u>másk</u> from árt class.

3. Sám the Mán is on the <u>lám</u>.

4. Háve a sándwich. Hám, <u>spám</u> or <u>lámb</u>?

VOCABULARY

<u>másk</u>	/mæsk/	A face made of paper or cloth that can be put on and off.
<u>on the lám</u>	/ʔan ðə læm/	To run away from the authorities.
<u>spám</u>	/spæm/	A mixture of meat, fat and other products pressed into a block. It's like a sausage without the skin.
<u>lámb</u>	/læm/	A baby sheep, the animal that provides us with wool.

FIND /æ/ IN THIS LIMERICK

Thrée <u>nánnies</u> were púshing their <u>práms</u>

When óne <u>tót</u> <u>took óff</u> on the lám.

Nánnie Gránt, in a fíx-ter,

Dashed áfter the trískster

And drágged it back hóme to its <u>Mám</u>.

VOCABULARY

<u>nánny</u>	/næni/	Someone who takes care of little children for pay.
<u>prám</u>	/præm/	Short for perambulator. A British word for baby carriage.
<u>tót</u>	/tat/	Short for toddler, a child between 1 & 3 years old.
<u>took óff</u>	/tUkɔ́f/	An idiom which is a synonym for ran away.
<u>Mam</u>	/mæm/	Another word for Mother or Mom.

FIND /æ/ IN THIS LIMERICK

A <u>Nánking</u> nanny named Náncy

<u>Nail</u>ed a táll man who <u>strúck her fáncy</u>.

She <u>núzzled</u> his néck.

He <u>fléd</u>, a tótal wréck,

As Náncy <u>decríed</u> his <u>inconstáncy</u>.

VOCABULARY

<u>Nánking</u>	/nǽnkiŋ/	A city in China.
<u>nail</u>	/nel/	To force others to do what you want them to do.
<u>struck her fancy</u>	/strʌ́k hUr fǽnsi/	Someone who looks very attractive.
<u>nuzzle</u>	/nʌ́zəl/	Rubbing one's face into someone else's neck.
<u>fled</u>	/flɛd/	The past tense of fly, to run away.
<u>decry</u>	/dikrái/	To complain loudly about something or someone's action.
<u>incónstancy</u>	/?InkánstInsi/	Unreliable. The change in SYLLABLE STRESS to /?Inkanstǽnsi/ is so that the word will rhyme with Náncy.

FIND /æ/ IN THESE RIDDLES

Which ánimal has the bést áccess to the tréetops?

A GIRAFFE

Which ánimal "backs" up to Páradise?

A CAMEL.

It's "back" (hump) points to the sky.

FIND /æ/ IN THIS STREET RHYME

Anna Banána

Pláys the piána (piano).

All she knèws

Is The Stár Spángled Bánna (Bánner).

FIND /æ/ IN THIS DOGGEREL

Pát-a-cake, pát-a-cake, báker's mán.

Báke me a cáke as fást as you cán.

Pát it and príck it and márk it with D.

Then pút it in the óven for Dílly and me.

FIND /æ/ IN THE DIALOGUE

LEVEL I: AN /æ/ DIALOGUE: THE CAT'S IN THE BAG

Anne: Andy! Lóok! That bág is móving!

Andy: Thát cán't bé!

Anne: I'm góing to exámine it. Andy! Look! It's a cát!

Andy: A cát? It múst be a véry fát one.

Anne: It's a black pánther!

Andy: A whát?! Anne, it cán't be a black pánther!

Anne: It's a bláck pánther cub, Ándy.

Andy: By golly, it is! And its báck legs are ínjured!

Anne: Let's ásk that párk atténdant for a hánd.

Andy: An ádmirable idea.

VOCABULARY

pánther	/pǽnθUr/	A leopard-type cat. Black panthers inhábit (live in) Sub-Saharan Africa, Asia and South Asia.
cub	/kʌb/	An infant or baby leopard.
a hánd	/ʔ ə hǽnd/	To ask for or give help.

Figure 20.

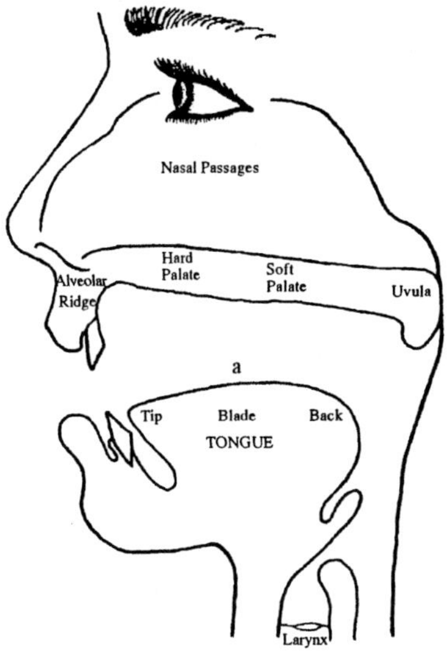

TO ARTICULATE SHORT /a/

1. Relax your jaw and say: AHHHH
2. Drop your tongue to the bottom of your mouth.

NOTE: MUCH OF THE TIME ALPHABET LETTER o IS PRONOUNCED /a/!

SPEAKING & PHONEME WRITING EXERCISES: short, relaxed /a/

1. Ah! A gólf hóliday!
2. The cót is in the cóttage.
3. Whát concóction are you cóoking up nów?
4. Dón't follow Lónnie. He hóbnobs with snóbs.
5. Móm! Cónnie is hot!

VOCABULARY

gólf	/galf/	An outdoor game played with curved sticks (clubs). The goal is to hit a small ball over a long distance into a hole in the ground.
cót	/kat/	A narrow bed that can be folded up and put in a closet.
cóttage	/kátIǰ/	A small, one-story house with 1 or 2 rooms.
concóction	/kənkákšIn/	A mixture of unknown or unusual things, usually foods.
hóbnob	/hábnab/	Associating with a group of people on a regular basis.
snób	/snab/	Someone who looks down on other people and is impolite.
hot	/hat/	A synonym for a fever.

FIND /a/ IN THIS RHYME

Chop, chóp, chóppity-chop.

Cút off the bóttom, cút off the tóp.

Whát is léft we'll pút in the pót.

Chóp, chóp, chóppity-chop.

FIND /a/ IN THIS LIMERICK

A <u>fóx</u> saw an <u>ótter</u> in a ríver,

Swímming <u>mérrily</u> with náry a shíver.

The fóx, so <u>enchánted</u>,

Jumped óff the <u>embánkment</u>,

To be <u>réscued</u> by Otter, his <u>delíverer</u>.

VOCABULARY

<u>fóx</u>	/faks/	A reddish, dog-like animal.
<u>ótter</u>	/?átUr/	A black, beaver-like animal with a body like a seal.
<u>mérrily</u>	/mέrIli/	With great joy and fun.
<u>náry</u>	/néri/	Without any at all.
<u>enchánted</u>	/?ɛnčǽntId/	Delighted and mesmerized (mágicked).
<u>embánkment</u>	/?ɛmbǽηkmInt/	The high bank or edge of a river.
<u>réscued</u>	/rɛskyud/	To be saved from danger.
<u>delíverer</u>	/dilÍvUrUr/	The one who saves you from danger.

FIND /a/ IN THIS TONGUE-TWISTER

Swan, swam óver the sea,

Swím, swan, swím!

Swán swam báck óver the sea.

Well swúm, swan!

VOCABULARY

swan	/swan/	A large, white, long-necked water bird that doesn't speak.
swím	/swIm/	The present tense form. Swam is the past tense form, and swúm is the past participle.

FIND /a/ IN THIS RHYME

Hóp, hóp, híppity hop.

Up from the bóttom,

Out from the tóp.

Píck up the pót.

Ooo! The pót's too hót!

Hóp, hóp, híppity hop.

Figure 21. Low Back Short Relaxed /a/.

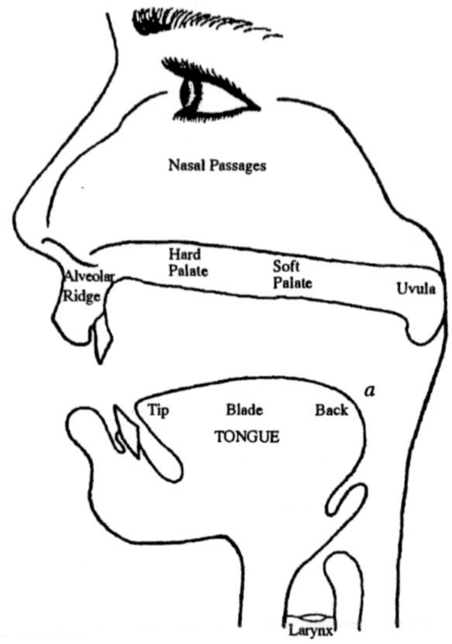

TO ARTICULATE short /a/

1. Pull the tongue back and down below the throat's opening.
2. Then relax the back of the tongue.

SPEAKING & PHONEME WRITING EXERCISES: short, relaxed /a/

1. Mártha's cár is márvelous.

2. The treé's bárk is scárred.

3. Párdon me. Are yóu Cármen McArthur?

4. Cálm down. Áuntie ónly stárched your scárf.

5. Cúpid's dart has hít my héart!

NOTE: AUNTIE can be pronounced three different ways: /?ǽnti/, /?ánti/, and /?*á*nti/. All three pronounciations are correct.

VOCABULARY

márvelous	/m*á*rvələs/	A synonym for wonderful, excellent, outstanding.
bárk	/b*a*rk/	The outer skin of a tree.
scár	/sk*a*r/	A deep cut that leaves a permanent mark on the skin.
stárch	/st*a*rc/	Flour mixed with water which will stiffen cloth (make it rigid or hard).
Cúpid	/kyúpId/	A baby Roman god whose arrows could make people love each other.
dart	/d*a*rt/	A small, narrow arrow.

FIND /æ/ & /a/ & /*a*/ IN THIS RHYME

Stánding at the bár,

Smóking a cigár,

Láughing like a dónkey,

Hár, hár hár.

FIND /*a*/ IN THIS LIMERICK

An ártist named Cármen McArthur,

Planned a gárden with an éxtra-large árbor.

The árch was só large,

That it spánned the garáge,

And dárkened the forest of Arden.

VOCABULARY

árbor	/ʔ*á*rbUr/	An large open-air room made of bent poles. They are found in gardens and are covered with climbing plants, such as roses or grapes.
arch	/ʔ*a*rč/	Similar to an arbor, an arch has a curved ceiling. An arch is usually constructed of stone. It cannot let in air or light through the ceiling like an arbor.
spanned	/spænd/	Spread across the entire length.

SPELLING:PRONUNCIATION NOTE

The /*a*/ PHONEME in American English is usually found in words where ALPHABET LETTER a is usually followed by ALPHABET LETTER r.

EXAMPLES: car park hard márket ártist fármer large

PHONEMES:

FIND /æ/ & /a/ & /*a*/ IN THESE PROVERBS

A hándful of <u>állies</u> <u>surpáss</u>es a wágon of góld.

Práctice makes skíllful.

You cán't unscrámble éggs.

Grátitude is nót the príce of chárity.

When <u>áardvark</u>s báttle, ánts appláud.

One hand wáshes the óther.

VOCABULARY

<u>áardvark</u>	/ʔ*á*rdv*a*rk/	An anteater from Africa.
<u>állies/ally</u>	/ʔælaiz/	People who support you.
<u>surpáss</u>	/sUrpǽs/	To go beyond the limits.

FIND /*a*/ IN THIS RHYME

Dówn with the lámbs,

Up with the lárk.

Gó to bed chíldren,

Befóre it gets dárk.

FIND /*a*/ IN THIS RHYME

Hárk, hárk, the dógs do bárk,

The béggars are cóming to tówn.

Sóme in rágs, sème in jágs,

And óne in a vélvet gówn.

VOCABULARY

jags /ǰægz/ Clothing that is cut in points.

FIND /*a*/ IN THESE 2 RHYMES

Bárber, bárber, sháve a pig.

Hów mány háirs to máke a wíg?

Chárley, Chárley, stóle the bárley,

Out of the shóp of Mr. Márley.

FIND /*a*/ IN THIS DOGGEREL

The Quéen of Héarts, she báked some tárts,

All on a súmmer's day.

The Kháve of Héarts, he stóle the tárts,

And tóok them cléan awáy.

VOCABULARY

tárts /t*a*rts/ Small fruit or meat pies.

LEVEL I: AN /a/ DIALOGUE: CARLA'S CARPET

Carla:	Hárvey! Stop! Dón't stárt the cár!
Harvey:	Why nót, Cárla?
Carla:	Our bárgain cárpet's júst arríved.
Harvey:	But I wánt to píck up my guitár!
Carla:	Hárv, dón't árgue! I wánt you hére!
Harvey:	Yóu are a márvelous óverséer, Carla. You dón't need me.
Carla:	Hárv, the cárpet comes fírst.
Harvey:	Cárla, the repáir shop clóses at fíve!
Carla:	It's ónly one o'clóck, Hárvey!
Harvey:	Yóu are ríght. I can píck up my guitár láter.

VOCABULARY

óverséer /?óvUrsíyUr/ Someone who supervises others' work. The boss.

FIND /æ/ & /a/ & /a/ IN THIS DIALOGUE

LEVEL II/III: AN /æ/ & /a/ & /a/ TRIALOGUE: SANDY, CONNIE AND CARL

Sandy: Who párked that lárge Cámry in the míddle of the blóck?

Carl: Í did. I'm stácking some bággage on the páth.

Connie: Sándy, Cárl and I néed a hánd.

Sandy: But you're blócking the ávenue!

Connie: Cálm dówn. Lét's táckle the bággage fírst.

Carl: Aunt Háttie and Fáther will be dríving úp soon.

Connie: Lét's not brángle.

Sandy: Sórry. Sáy, thát's an áwful lót of bággage.

Carl: Wé're óccupying the lárge apártment óver the garáge.

Sandy: Why dóesn't ányone téll me ánything?

VOCABULARY

stáck	/stæk/	To put one box or package on top of another.
táckle	/tǽkəl/	To start a job and finish it without a break.
bággage	/bǽgIǰ/	Bags people carry with them when they travel.
brángle	/brǽngəl/	A fussy argument.

VOWEL PHONEME:SPELLING REVIEW I

/æ/ & /a/ & /*a*/

FIND /æ/ & /a/ & /*a*/ IN THESE EXERCISES

SPEAKING & PHONEME WRITING CONTRAST EXERCISES: /æ/ & /a/ & /*a*/

1. Cónnie hággled óver the váse.
2. The pót's crácked.
3. I wánt that lárge bóttle.
4. Bárgain with the shópkeeper.
5. Márvin sát on my hát!
6. Cán't we móp the bár?
7. He wánts to wásh the wálrus.
8. The pásta's on the táble.

VOCABULARY

hággle	/hǽgəl/	To argue or bárgain down the price of an item.
vase	/v*a*z/ or /vez/	A tall container which holds cut flowers.
wálrus	/wálrəs/	A large sea animal, like a seal.
pásta	/pástə/	The Italian word for all types of spaghetti.

FIND /æ/ & /a/ IN THIS RHYME

Sálly go róund the sún,

Sálly go róund the móon.

Sálly go róund the chímney póts,

On a Sáturday áfternóon.

VOWEL PHONEME:SPELLING REVIEW II

/æ/ & /a/ & */a/*

FILL IN THE SPACES UNDER THE ALPHABET LETTERS WITH WORDS FROM THE EXERCISES AND THEIR PHONEMES.

PHONEMES:	/æ/	/a/	*/a/*			
ALPHABET LETTERS:	a	oC	aC(C)/eaC(C)			
			ar	alm	ant/ash	ear
AL:	práctice chat	hot pot	car	calm	want/wash	heart
PH:						
AL:	nánny drag	Cónnie	Carl	palm		
PH:						
AL:	Spam lamb	cóttage				
PH:						
AL:	pram can					
PH:						
AL:	Aunt	Aunt			Aunt	
PH:						
AL:						
PH:						
AL:						
PH:						
AL:						
PH:						
AL:						
PH:						

oC — ALPHABET LETTER o sounds like /a/ when it is followed by one or more consonants: cop, bóttom, knock, cómpromise.

aCC — ALPHABET LETTER a sounds like */a/* most of the time when followed by ALPHABET LETTER r: farm, pártner, and also when followed by ALPHABET LETTER 1: palm, calm, psalm.

eaC(C) — ALPHABET LETTER COMBINATION ear often sounds like */a/*: heart.

THE TWO MID-CENTRAL VOWELS: SHORT DELTA /Λ/ & SHORTER SCHWA /ə/

TO ARTICULATE DELTA /Λ/

1. Drop your jaw.
2. Drop your tongue.
3. Constrict the glottis (vocal cords).

TO ARTICULATE SCHWA /ə/

1. Swallow the back of your tongue. Then gulp.
2. SCHWA is even shorter than /Λ/.

Figure 22.

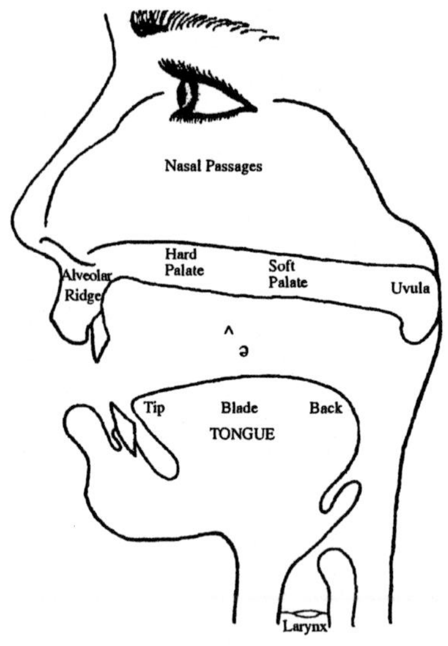

SPEAKING & PHONEME WRITING CONTRAST EXERCISES: /Λ/ & /ə/

short delta /Λ/	shorter schwa /ə/
1a. A <u>búndle</u> of únwashed únderwear.	1b. Bútton up, Amánda.
2a. Bettína's upsét abóut Búddy	2b. Come alóng with ús.
3a. The <u>púddle</u>'s múddy.	3b. A <u>cóuple</u> of púppies.
4a. <u>Dóuble</u> or nóthing.	4b. Búddy's <u>múm</u>bling.

5. Dón't <u>tróuble</u> tróuble till tróuble tróubles you.

NOTE: There is a group of TWO-SYLLABLE WORDS that carry BOTH SHORT DELTA /Λ/ & SHORTER SCHWA /ə/. A few examples are:
<u>búndle</u> /bΛ́ndəl/ <u>púddle</u> /pΛ́dəl/ <u>múmble</u> /mΛ́mbəl/
<u>cóuple</u> /kΛ́pəl/ <u>dóuble</u> /dΛ́bəl/ <u>tróuble</u> /trΛ́bəl/
For SYLLABIC /əl/, see Chapter III, page 123.

FIND DELTA /Λ/ & SCHWA /ə/ IN THESE RHYMES

AN /Λ/ & /ə/ DOGGEREL

Húmpty Dúmpty sát on a wáll.

Húmpty Dúmpty hád a great fáll.

All the king's hórses and áll the kíng's men,

Cóuldn't put Húmpty togéther agáin.

A DOGGEREL is English rhyme for passing gossip anonymously (nameless). In 15th & 16th century England, courtiers (nobles) in Henry VIII, Mary I and Elizabeth I's courts could spread personal & political information without putting themselves in danger. Doggerels are so entertaining that they appear today as children's nursery rhymes.

Humpty Dumpty was a knickname (another name) for the Earl of Essex. He tried to force Queen Elizabeth I to marry him. He wanted to become King of England. Instead, he was sentenced to the Tower for treason & lost his head (his head was chopped off).

AN /Λ/ & /ə/ LIMERICK

A tróublesome trío from Dúblin,

All grúbby and chúbby and fúmblin',

Turned óut their póckets for chánge,

For they wánted to arránge

A bús trip to metropólitan Lóndon.

VOCABULARY

grúbby	/grΛ́bi/	Somewhat dirty, with messy, not-very-clean clothes.
chúbby	/čΛ́bi/	Not quite fat. Plump.
fúmbling	/fΛ́mbliŋ/	Touches an object and it falls over. Clumsiness.

FIND /Λ/ IN THIS DOGGEREL

Old Móther Húbbard, wént to the cúpboard

To fínd her póor dog a bóne.

But whén she got thére, the cúpboard was báre,

And só, the póor dog had nóne.

VOCABULARY

cúpboard	/kΛ́bUrd/	A pantry or closet for food.

FIND /Λ/ IN THIS RHYME

A skúnk was drúmming in the lócal pub,

His bróther was drúmming there, tóo.

They drúmmed so lóng that sómeone erúpted,

Condémning the húbbub as abúse.

VOCABULARY

skunk	/skΛnk/	A small black-furred animal with a white stripe down its back. When frightened or angry, it emits a terrible stench (smell).
pub	/pΛb/	A public house or bar.
erúpted	/?IrΛ́ptId/	Blew up. Became very angry.
condémn	/kəndɛ́m/	To call something evil and act to destroy it.
húbbub	/hΛ́bΛb/	Noise and commotion.
abúse	/?əbyús/	Harming someone who is helpless.

FIND DELTA /Λ/ & SCHWA /ə/ IN THIS DIALOGUE

LEVEL I/II: AN /Λ/ & /ə/ DIALOGUE: MUFFIN & BUBBLES

Bubbles: My dúmb bróther Túffy's cóming to súpper.

Muffin: Búbbles! Dón't cáll your bróther dúmb!

Bubbles: A cóuple of his <u>búddies</u> are cóming, tóo.

Muffin: You shóuld have <u>alért</u>ed me sóoner.

Bubbles: There's some <u>mútton</u> <u>stew</u> and <u>potáto puffs</u>.

Muffin: Wéll, they'll júst have to táke <u>potlúck</u>.

Bubbles: Dídn't you píck up some <u>húshpuppies</u> and púdding éarlier?

Muffin: Yúp. Forgót abóut them. Nów we have enóugh <u>grub</u>.

VOCABULARY

<u>búddies</u>	/bΛ́diz/	A synonym for close friends.
<u>alért</u>	/?əlÚrt/	To be on guard, to be notified.
<u>mútton</u>	/mΛ́tIn/	The meat from a mature sheep.
<u>stew</u>	/stu/	A thick, cooked mixture of all kinds of foods.
<u>potáto puffs</u>	/pətétə pΛfs/	Mashed potatoes mixed with spices and fried.
<u>potlúck</u>	/pátlΛ́k/	Eat what is available.
<u>húshpuppies</u>	/hΛ́špèpiz/	A deep-fried mixture cornmeal, eggs & spices.
<u>grub</u>	/grΛ́b/	A slang (street-speech) word for food.

REVIEW NOTE

ALPHABET LETTER U sounds like /Λ/ in many single-syllable words (grub) and when its syllable is stressed (búbble).

FIND DELTA /ʌ/ & SCHWA /ə/ IN THIS DIALOGUE

LEVEL I/II: AN /ʌ/ & /ə/ DIALOGUE: THE LUGGAGE ON THE BUS

Bud: Stóp that bús! My móther left her lúggage on that bús!

Judd: How frústrating!

Bud: I've gót to búzz the bús cómpany. Whére's a télephone?

Judd: The bús dépot's júst aróund the córner.

Bud: Whát great lúck! Thánks!

Judd: Í'd call it a tóuch of dúmb lúck.

Bud: Áll too trúe. Ý the wáy, whát's your náme?

Judd: Júdd. What's yóurs?

Bud: Búd. Sée you aróund, Júdd.

Judd: Sée you aróund, Búd.

VOCABULARY

luggage	/lʌ́gIǰ/	Baggage.
frustrating	/frʌ́stretiŋ/	Not being able to do what you want to do.
buzz	/bʌ́z/	Telephoning someone.
depot	/dípo/	A large parking lot for buses.

3 VOWEL PHONEME:SPELLING NOTES ON EXTRA-SHORT SCHWA /ə/

1. Syllablic /əl/ 2. The Indefinite Article a
3. Unstressed Alphabet Letter a

1. SYLLABIC /əl/

When an unaccented syllable ends in /l/, the vowel is nearly always SCHWA /ə/, the vowel:consonant combination for SYLLABIC /əl/.

SPEAKING & PHONEME WRITING EXAMPLES: /əl/

a. My sándal's unbúckled.

b. Mérrill is véry cápable.

c. Dón't stúmble.

d. The bágel is crúmbling!

NOTE: See Chapter III, page 123 for SYLLABIC /əl/ & page 46 for examples.

2. The INDEFINITE ARTICLE a is supposed to be pronounced /ʔə/. But, people often articulate INDEFINITE ARTICLE a as /ʔe/. They do that to communicate at least 4 items of information, often all at the same time.

   a. They are deliberately pronouncing /ʔe/ rather than /ʔə/ to make it very clear the attached noun phrase is special.

   b. The speaker may also be signalling that it is not finished speaking.

   c. Articulating /ʔe/ can signal listeners that the speaker is searching for the right word.

   d. Sometimes pronouncing /ʔe/ instead of /ʔə/ indicates that the speaker intends to dominate the conversation.

SPEAKING & PHONEME WRITING CONTRAST EXAMPLES:

/ʔə/	/ʔe/
a. Í have a hát.	b. Í have á hát.
d. Gíve him a kítten.	e. Gíve him á kítten.

3. Whenever a word begins with the ALPHABET LETTER a and stress is on another syllable, ALPHABET LETTER a is pronounced /ʔə/.

SPEAKING & PHONEME WRITING EXAMPLES:

a. Anóther annóuncement?

b. Bén arríved on tíme.

c. The théater áudience appláuded.

d. Climb abóard, Olívia.

THE FOUR BACK HIGH, HIGH-MID, MID & MID-LOW VOWELS

/u/ & /U/ AND /o/ & /ɔ/

Figure 23.

LONG BACK HIGH TENSE /u/

SHORT BACK HIGH-MID /U/

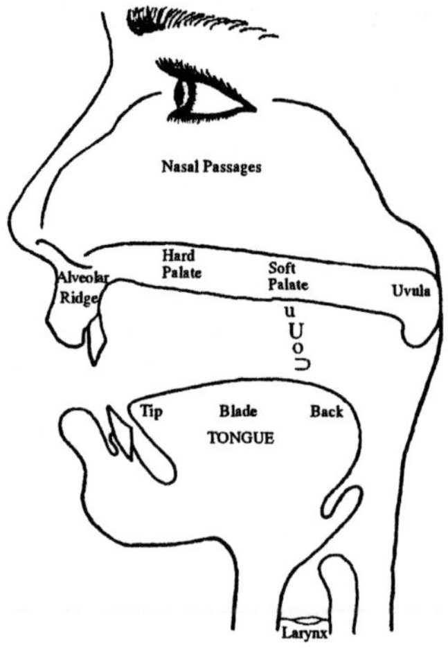

LONG BACK MID TENSE /o/

LONG BACK MID-LOW /ɔ/

Figure 24.

TO ARTICULATE /u/

1. Raise your tongue to the /i/ position (see page 18).
2. Purse your lips (kiss the baby).

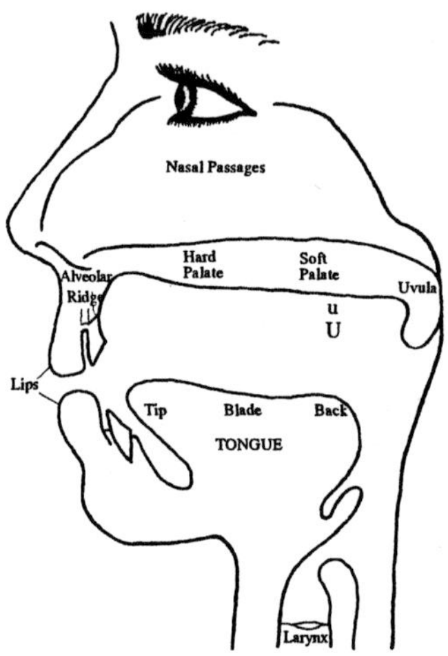

SPEAKING & PHONEME WRITING CONTRAST EXERCISES: /u/ & /U/

long, tense /u/

1. The nóodles are cóoling.
2. Dó impróve your mood.
3. My <u>néw</u> flúte is beaútiful.
4. I dréw a blue <u>raccóon</u>.

short, relaxed /U/

1. Pút your fóot in the bóot.
2. Cóokie's a <u>cróok</u>.
3. The bóok's in the bóokbag.
4. What a góod cookie!

VOCABULARY

<u>crook</u>	/krUk/	A thief.
<u>raccoon</u>	/rækún/	An small animal with a black mask around its eyes.

NOTE: See Chapter III, pages 176–178 for Invisible y & <u>/nu/nyu/</u> patterns.

FIND /u/ & /U/ IN THIS LIMERICK

A flútist who tóoted and tútored,

Grew tíred of mínimum lúcre.

She tóok up her túcker

And fléw to Bankók-er

Where she retóoled and becáme a trúcker.

VOCABULARY

flútist	/flútIst/	Someone who plays the flute.
lúcre	/lúkUr/	A synonym for money.
túcker	/tÁkUr/	An Australian word for food.
Bankók	/bæŋkák/	The capitol city of Thailand (Siam).
retóoled	/ritúld/	Retrained.
trúcker	/trÁkUr/	Someone who drives a truck, an eighteen-wheeler.

FIND /u/ & /U/ IN THIS DOGGEREL

Póor óld Róbinson Crúsoe!

Póor óld Róbinson Crúsoe!

He máde him a cóat,

Of an óld nánny góat.

Póor óld Róbinson Crúsoe!

VOCABULARY

Róbinson Crúsoe	/rábInsIn krúso/	Daniel DeFoe's shipwrecked hero.

FIND /u/ & /U/ & /Λ/ IN THIS RHYME

The nóodles are cóol,

The stéw is, tóo.

To téll the trúth,

I dón't gíve a hóot.

VOCABULARY

stew	/stu/ or /styu/	A very thick soup.
gíve a hóot	/gívə hút/	I don't care.

AN /U/ TONGUE TWISTER

While I dózed by the bróok,

A cróok tóok my bóok.

Would the cróok have hóoked my bóok,

Had I béen on the lóok?

VOCABULARY

dozed	/dozd/	To fall into a light sleep.
brook	/brUk/	A stream or narrow river where the water tumbles over rocks.
crook	/krUk/	A thief or robber.
hooked	/hUkt/	Grabbed.
on the look	/ʔán ðə lÚk/	To be aware and awake.

FIND /U/ & /Λ/ IN THIS RHYME

How much wóod would a wóodchuck chúck

If a wóodchuck cóuld chuck wóod?

VOCABULARY

wóodchuck	/wUdčΛk/	Another name for a groundhog. It lives in a burrow, an underground tunnel.
chuck	/čΛk/	A synonym for chop.

FIND /U/ & /Λ/ IN THIS DOGGEREL

Hére is Súlky Súe.

Whát are wé to dó?

Túrn her fáce to the wáll,

Tíll she comes tó.

FIND /U/ & /Λ/ IN THIS RHYME

A blúe moon ríses ónly in Júne,

Whén the dógwood dróps its fíve-pétaled blóoms.

Whén shóoting stárs frólic thróugh my háir,

Máking eléctric the dárk night áir.

VOCABULARY

dógwood	/dɔ́gwUd/	A small tree that blooms in the spring.
frólic	/frálIk/	To play and have fun.

FIND LONG /u/ & SHORT /U/ IN THIS DIALOGUE

LEVEL I: AN /u/ & /U/ DIALOGUE: SUZIE & COOKIE

Cookie:	Súzie, where áre you?
Suzie:	In the blúe room, Cóokie. What's dóing?
Cookie:	I júst púrchased a néw súit. Try it ón.
Suzie:	You knów I dón't like súits.
Cookie:	It's a blúe one, Súzie.
Suzie:	My fávorite <u>húe</u>.
Cookie:	Dó lóok at it.
Suzie:	I'm nót in the móod.
Cookie:	Dón't be <u>rúde</u>, Sue.
Suzie:	Ókay. Pút it on the stóol.
Cookie:	Póoh!

VOCABULARY

<u>húe</u>	/hyu/	A shade or variation of a color.
<u>rude</u>	/rud/	To be impolite.

LEVEL I/II: AN /u/ & /U/ DIALOGUE: LULU'S COOKBOOK

Lulu:	Luke! Look! My new cóokbook!
Luke:	LULU'S COOKIE COOKBOOK. The títle looks gréat, Lúlu!
Lulu:	Do you réally líke the títle?
Luke:	It sóunds júst like yóu.
Lulu:	The <u>récipes</u> are prétty góod, too.
Luke:	I óught to knów. I'm <u>hóoked</u> on your cóokies, Lu.
Lulu:	Lúke, yóu are a fóol for fóod.
Luke:	Júst a fóol for your cóokies.
Lulu:	<u>Kúdos</u> will gét you cóokies.
Luke:	Góod. Whén's the néxt <u>bátch</u>?
Lulu:	Soon.

VOCABULARY

<u>récipe</u>	/résIpi/	A written explanation of how to cook a particular dish.
<u>hooked</u>	/hUkt/	To became dependent on.
<u>kúdo</u>	/kúdo/	A compliment.
<u>batch</u>	/bæč/	A collection or group of things.

VOWEL PHONEME:SPELLING REVIEW II

/u/ & /U/

FILL IN THE SPACES UNDER THE ALPHABET LETTERS WITH WORDS FROM THE EXERCISES AND THEIR PHONEMES.

PHONEMES:	/u/					/yu/		/U/			
ALPHABET LETTERS:	oo	o/wo	uCe	ui/ue	ough	ew/eu	uCe	oo	oul	uC(C)	or
AL:	boot	to/two	flute	suit	through	new	cute	cook	could	put	worse
PH:											
AL:	too		tune	glue		stew	mule	look	would	push	work
PH:											
AL:	food					few		took	should		word
PH:											
AL:	moon					cue		book			world
PH:											
AL:											
PH:											
AL:											
PH:											
AL:											
PH:											
AL:											
PH:											
AL:											
PH:											

uCe — /u/ is one of the sounds for this combination of ALPHABET LETTERS.

uCe — Another sound is /yu/, as in cute, mute, mule, immúre (to bury alive).

uC(C) — A small set of words fits this pattern. cúshion, push, put.

or — There are a number of ALPHABET VOWEL + r combinations that sound like /Ur/. See Chapter III, pages 132–134, the 3 SYLLABIC /r/.

THE TWO LONG BACK HIGH-MID:MID-LOW VOWELS

LONG /o/ & LONG /⊃/

Figure 25.

TO ARTICULATE /o/
1. Drop your jaw.
2. Then purse your lips (kiss the baby).

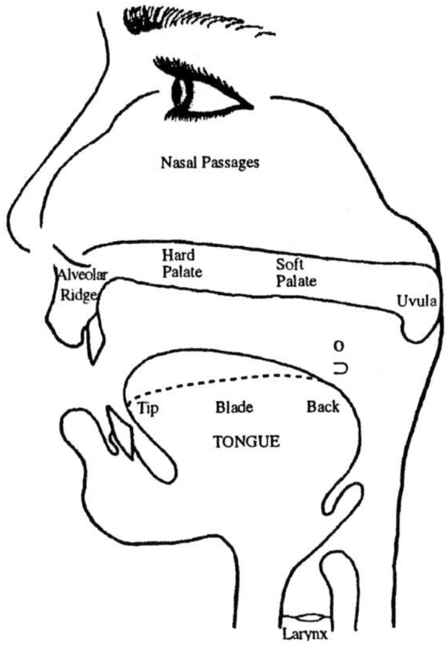

TO ARTICULATE /⊃/
1. Drop your tongue.
2. Drop your jaw.

SPEAKING & PHONEME WRITING CONTRAST EXERCISES: LONG /o/ & LONG /⊃/

long /o/	long /⊃/
1. Séw your cóat.	1. I bóught some cóffee.
2. Hóld the phóne.	2. He bóught a <u>flóral órnament</u>.
3. My nóse is cóld.	3. More cóffee, Paul?
4. Dón't flóat the bóat.	4. The <u>sháwl</u>'s caught.

VOCABULARY

<u>flóral órnament</u>	/fl⊃́rə l⊃́rnəmInt/	A decoration made of flowers.
<u>shawl</u>	/š⊃l/	A large square cloth that you wear around your shoulders.

FIND LONG /o/ & SHORT /Λ/ IN THIS RHYME

Hére am I, Líttle Júmping Jóan.

When nóbody's wíth me, I'm áll alóne.

AN /u/ & /o/ LIMERICK

Twó fóols went to séa in a bóat.

Both negléctted to bríng alóng a cóat.

They fróze stíff as státues,

Iced óver like gáteaus.

Now they're bóuys that óther ships nóte.

VOCABULARY

negléct	/nIglέkt/	To forget about or ignore doing something.
gatéaus	/gǽtuz/	A French word for a small glazed cake.
bouys	/b⊃iz/	From French. Floats in the water wherever there are boats.

FIND /⊃/ IN THIS RHYME

Nót last níght, but the níght befóre,

Twénty-four róbbers knócked at my dóor.

Í ran óut, théy ran ín,

So I tápped their héads with a rólling pin.

VOCABULARY

rólling pin	/róliη pIn/	A short, thick, round stick for rolling out dough.

AN /⊃/ DOGGEREL

Jérry Háll, he's só small,

A rát could éat him, hát and áll.

FIND LONG /o/ & LONG /ɔ/ & SHORT /ʌ/ IN THIS DOGGEREL

Líttle Jack Hórner, sát in a córner,

Eating a dámson pie.

He pút in his thúmb, and púlled out a plúm

Then sáid: "Whát a góod boy am I!"

VOCABULARY

dámson /dǽmsIn/ A kind of plum.

AN /ɔ/ DOGGEREL

It's ráining, it's póuring,

The óld man is snóring.

He wént to béd, and búmped his héad

And cóuldn't get úp in the mórning!

FIND /o/ & /ɔ/ IN THIS RHYME

Thrée wise mén named Cole,

Rán to séa in a bówl.

If the bówl were strónger,

My sóng would be lónger.

LEVEL I/II: AN /o/ & /ɔ/ DIALOGUE: TOTIE & SAUL

Saul: Tótie, wíll you séw the sléeve of my cóat?

Totie: Séw it yoursélf, Sául.

Saul: Oh, áll ríght! Whére's the séwing kit?

Totie: I stówed it in the álcove of your wálk-in clóset.

Saul: Oh, nó! Tótie, how cóuld you? You knów I'm cláustrophóbic!

Totie: Just móve the cóats asíde. It's clóse to the óutside córner.

Saul: Oh, gróss! What an áwful féeling!

Totie: Now clóse the dóor.

Saul: I knów, I knów. Tótie, dón't do that agáin.

Totie: I wón't. Sórry, Sául.

VOCABULARY

álcove	/ʔǽlkov/	A nook or cavity.
cláustrophóbic	/klɔ́strəfóbIk/	A word from psychology. To be afraid of close spaces.
gross	/gros/	Disgusting, offensive, very unpleasant.

FIND LONG /o/ & LONG /⊃/ IN THIS DIALOGUE

LEVEL II/III: AN /o/ & /⊃/ DIALOGUE: TONY & PAUL

Tony: Pául, I néed a láwyer.

Paul: I knów. I héard you dróve a hóle ínto a stóre wíndow.

Tony: Who tóld you?

Paul: Chlóris.

Tony: I could chóke her.

Paul: Don't be sílly. Téll me áll.

Tony: I had júst walked óut of Mauríce's hárdware store.

Paul: Gó on.

Tony: I bóught a síx-fóot pole with which to páint the háll walls.

Paul: Só?

Tony: Twó cóeds on róllerblades jólted my árm.

Paul: Dón't tell me. You..........

Tony: Póked a hóle through the stóre window.

FIND /u/ & /U/ AND /o/ & /⊃/ IN THIS DIALOGUE

LEVEL I/II: AN /u/ & /U/ AND /o/ & /⊃/ DIALOGUE: SOUP OR STEW?

Stuart: Cóokie, I'm cóld. Is there ány sóup or stéw on the stóve?

Cookie: There's móre. Góulash, chícken broth, and a séafood chówder.

Stuart: What's góulash?

Cookie: It's a méat stew.

Stuart: How abóut a bówl of éach?

Cookie: Okáy. In what órder?

Stuart: Góulash, then bróth, then chówder.

Cookie: Stúart, you are the oríginal consúmer. An óveréater.

Stuart: You are tótally......... right!

Cookie: I'm álways right!

VOCABULARY

stew	/stu/ or /styu/	A thick soup made of meat and potatoes.
góulash	/gúlaˇ s/	A Hungarian meat stew with paprika.
broth	/br⊃θ/	The liquid from a soup minus the meat and vegetables.
chówder	/ˇ cáudUr/	A thick fish or seafood soup.

VOWEL PHONEME:SPELLING REVIEW

/o/ & /⊃/

FILL IN THE SPACES UNDER THE ALPHABET LETTERS WITH WORDS FROM THE EXERCISES AND THEIR PHONEMES.

PHONEMES:			/o/					/⊃/				
ALPHABET LETTERS:	oCe	oe	oa	ow/ew	ough	omb	oo	au/gh	ou/gh	aw	oCe	al/t
AL:	wrote	toe	boat	bow	though	comb	floor	caught	bought	law	fore	tall
PH:												
AL:	robe	flow	coat	sew			door		sought	áwful	more	all
PH:												
AL:	hope	grow	float	two								wáter
PH:												
AL:												
PH:												
AL:												
PH:												
AL:												
PH:												
AL:												
PH:												
AL:												
PH:												
AL:												
PH:												

oCe Here are 2 types of oCe ALPHABET LETTERS. The CONSONANT in the oCe, pronounced /⊃/, is most often an /r/: core, lore, sore, more, tore. The CONSONANTS in the oCe, pronounced /o/, are usually all the others, including /l/: cope, mole, note, sole, hope, home.

REVIEW EXERCISES FOR THE 13 VOWEL PHONEMES AND 3 DIPHTHONGS

FIND VOWEL AND DIPHTHONG PHONEMES IN THIS DOGGEREL

Mrs. Máson bóught a básin.

Mrs. Tyson said: "What a níce one!"

"Whát did it cóst?" asked Mrs. Fróst.

"Hálf-a-crown." ánswered Mrs. Brówn.

"Díd it, indéed?" queried Mrs. Réed.

"It díd for cértain." replíed Mrs. Cúrtain.

Then Mrs. Níx, úp to her trícks,

Thréw the básin ónto the brícks!

VOCABULARY

básin	/bésIn/	A large, metal bowl.
hálf-a-crówn	/hæfəkráun/	A British coin worth today about 75 cents.

FIND VOWEL PHONEMES IN THIS DOGGEREL

Síng a sóng of síxpence, a pócket full of rye.

Fóur and twénty bláckbirds báked in a píe.

Whén the píe was ópen, the bírds begán to síng.

Nów, wásn't thát a tásty dish to sét befóre the kíng.

VOCABULARY

síxpence	/sÍkspεns/	A British coin worth about 6 cents.
rye	/rai/	A grain like wheat and barley.

FIND THE VOWEL PHONEMES IN THESE RHYMES

Thírty days háth Septémber,

April, June and Novémber.

All the rést have thírty-one,

Excépting Fébruary alóne.

And thát has twénty-eight days cléar,

And twenty-níne in each léap year.

Mr. Eást gáve a feast,

Mr. Nórth láid the cloth.

Mr. Wést did his best,

Mr. Sóuth búrnt his mouth

While éating a cold potáto.

On Sáturday night I lóst my wife

And whére do you thínk I fóund her?

Up in the móon, sínging a túne,

And áll of the stars aróund her.

THE 3 DIPHTHONGS: /ai/ & /au/ & /ɔi/

Figure 26.

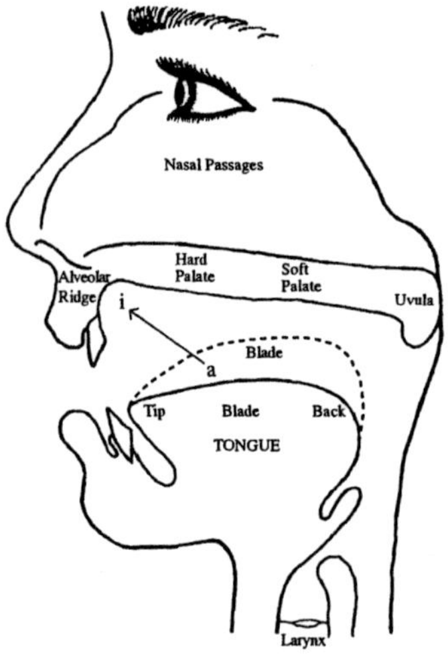

Figure 27.

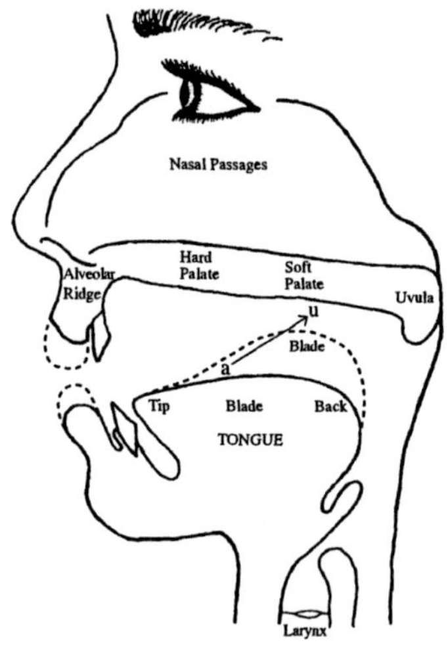

Figure 28.

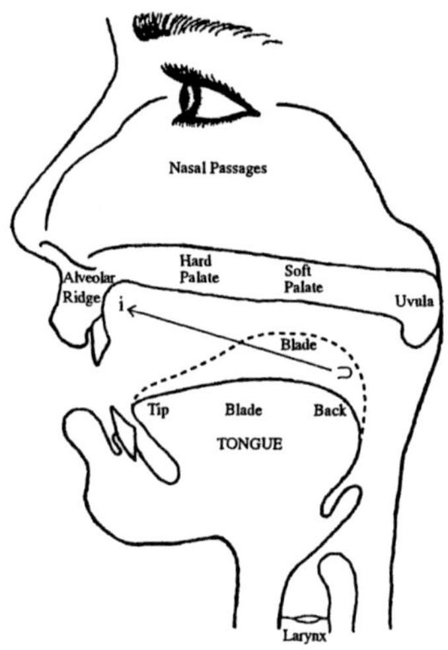

NOTE: DIPHTHONGS are combinations of 2 VOWEL PHONEMES. They do not allow a consonant to separate them. If a consonant does appear between 2 VOWEL PHONEMES, then the 2 vowels are really part of 2 syllables.

SPEAKING & PHONEME WRITING CONTRAST EXERCISES: /ai/ & /au/ & /ɔi/

1. Búy a flúffy móuse toy for Jóy.

2. Try to bé on tíme. We díne at fíve.

3. The clówn smíled shyly at the crying chíld.

4. The bóys scrounged aróund for tíny whíte míce.

5. Joy's boy is asléep for the níght.

VOCABULARY

scróunged /skráunǰd/ Looked for.

FIND THE /ai/ DIPHTHONG IN THIS RHYME

Stár light, stár bright,

Fírst star I sée tonight.

I wísh I máy, I wísh I míght,

Háve the wísh I wísh toníght.

FIND VOWELS & DIPHTHONG /ai/ IN THIS RIDDLE

As Í was góing to St. Íves,

I mét a mán with séven wíves.

Éach wife had séven sacks.

Each sáck held séven cats.

Each cát birthed séven kits.

Kits, cats, sacks, wives:

How mány were góing to St.Íves?

ANSWER: It depends. WIVES + SACKS + CATS + KITTENS + MAN = 7+7+7+7+1.

The riddle does not tell us the direction the narrator is travelling. Here are the possibilities.

1. The man alone. 1
2. The man, his wives, the sacks, cats and kits. 29
3. The man and the narrator. 2
4. The man, his wives, the sacks, cats, kits and the narrator. 30
5. Were any of the travelers riding horses? Then you would have to add them to the total as well!

FIND THE /ai/ DIPHTHONG IN THIS DOGGEREL

Thrée blind míce. Thrée blind míce.

Sée how they rún! Sée how they rún!

They áll ran áfter the fármer's wife.

She cút off their táils with a cárving knife.

Have you éver seen such a síght in your life

As thrée blind míce?

NOTE: When a diphthong precedes Liquids /r/ or /l/, Glides /w/ or /y/ usually separate the vowels, creating 2 syllables. See pages 77–78 in this chapter for when a diphthong is NOT a diphthong.

FIND /áyUr/ IN THIS RHYME

Our <u>chóir</u> <u>aspíred</u> to <u>acquíre</u> first príze.

So we <u>dúel</u>ed other chóirs,

Sínging the bést of óur líves.

VOCABULARY

<u>chóir</u>	/kwáyUr/	A group of people who sing together.
<u>aspíre</u>	/ʔəspáyUr/	To want a thing very badly.
<u>acquíre</u>	/ʔəkwáyUr/	To buy, earn or receive an object.

FIND THE /ai/ DIPHTHONG IN THIS DIALOGUE

LEVEL I: AN /ai/ DIALOGUE: IDA'S BICYCLE

Myra: Ída, my bícycle has júst arríved.

Ida: Is it anóther <u>rácer</u>?

Myra: Nó, it's a <u>móuntain bike</u>.

Ida: Nice línes! I lóve that lívely cólor.

Myra: Sápphire, my fávorite blue.

Ida: Why did you búy this bíke?

Myra: My whíte rácer ísn't cápable of clímbing hígh hills.

Ida: Yóu're ríght. I míght buy a móuntain bike, tóo.

Myra: Lét's try it óut.

Ida: Lét's!

VOCABULARY		
<u>rácer</u>	/résUr/	A light-weight bicycle with narrow tires.
<u>móuntain bike</u>	/máuntIn báik/	A heavy-duty bicycle with wide, sturdy tires.

FIND /au/ IN THIS RIDDLE

Whát weighs móre?

A póund of clówns or a póund of cóffee grounds?

NEITHER: BOTH WEIGH THE SAME: A POUND

FIND /au/ IN THIS RHYME

After a lóng caróuse,

The clówn was drówsy,

Her gówn all tóuseled,

And her mákeup all gróuty.

VOCABULARY

caróuse	/kəráuz/	A wild, crazy weekend.
drówsy	/dráuzi/	Very sleepy.
tóuseled	/táusəld/	Messy and torn.
gróuty	/gráuti/	Gritty with sand.

FIND /au/ IN THIS RHYME

How nów, bróusing brown ców.

'Tis tíme to plów the gróund enów.

VOCABULARY

bróusing	/bráuziŋ/	To graze or eat grass.
'tis	/tIz/	An old-fashioned pronunciation for It is.
plow	/plau/	To turn over the soil with a large hook pulled by an animal.
enów	/?ináu/	An old-fashioned word for presently.

FIND THE /au/ DIPHTHONG IN THIS DIALOGUE

LEVEL I: AN /au/ DIALOGUE: COUNT ME OUT

Gower: Cóunt me óut.

Howard: But Gówer, áll we're dóing is hóusing a móuse.

Gower: Cóunt them, Hóward. How abóut a thóusand?

Howard: We cán't just tóss them óut!

Gower: And you cánnot allów a thóusand míce to run lóose in the house!

Howard: Thát's why I'm cóunting on your hélp!

Gower: I cóunsel you to endów the zóo with those míce.

Howard: I'm a cóward, Gówer.

Gower: Dón't frown. I'll cáll the zóo for yóu.

Howard: Now?

Gower: Now.

VOCABULARY

cóunsel	/káunsəl/	To advise /?ədváiz/, to give someone advice /?ədváis/.
endów	/?ɛndáu/	To give as a gift. To donate.
frown	/fraun/	To wrinkle your forehead because you are angry.

AN /ɔi/ RHYME

An ásteroid drópped in the míddle of Bóise.

It máde so much nóise,

It drove éveryone cróizy (crazy).

VOCABULARY

Bóise	/bɔizi/	A city in Idaho.

FIND /ɔi/ IN THESE RIDDLES

1. Whát's the dífference betwéen a bóy and a tóy?

ONE BEGINS WITH "B," THE OTHER BEGINS WITH "T"

2. Why did the kói ignóre the cóin?

BECAUSE IT WAS COY

VOCABULARY

koi	/kɔi/	A domesticated fish.
coy	/kɔi/	To be cute and shy.

3. Why did the óyster embróider the dóily?

BECAUSE IT WAS BORED

VOCABULARY

óyster	/?ɔ́istUr/	A round shellfish often eaten raw.
embróider	/?ɛmbrɔ́idUr/	To sew a design in colored threads.
dóily	/dɔ́ili/	A small piece of crochét (openwork) to place on furniture.

FIND /⊃i/ IN THIS DIALOGUE

LEVEL I/II: AN /⊃i/ DIALOGUE: TOYA & ROY

Toya: Oh bóy, oh bóy!

Roy: Tóya, whát are you “oh bóying” abóut?

Toya: I bóught some kói from Hanói.

Roy: Whát’s the póint? The óther koi were destróyed.

Toya: They were póisoned, I knów.

Roy: Thése koi will móst líkely die, tóo.

Toya: I’ll avóid that by spóiling the póisoner’s plóy.

Roy: How?

Toya: We’ll hóuse the kói indóors.

Roy: Oy! Móre koi!

Toya: Stop spóiling my góod news. It’s annóying.

Roy: All ríght, Mádame Koi. Yóu win.

VOCABULARY

ploy /pl⊃y/ A sneaky trick.

LEVEL II: A TRIALOGUE: /ai/ & /au/ & /⊃i/: TYRONE, RAO & ROY

Rao: You're súch a sly bóy, Róy.

Roy: Why do you sáy such símple-minded thíngs?

Ty: Yóu two are álways spóiling for a fíght.

Roy: Wé try.

Rao: Quíte ríght.

Ty: Bé nice. We've míles to dríve befóre níghtfall.

Rao: What tíme will wé arríve?

Roy: Abóut níne, nine-thírty.

Ty: What tíme is it nów?

Roy: Four-thírty. Why?

Ty: Téa time, féllas. Lét's eat.

VOCABULARY

sly	/slai/	Clever, but untrustworthy.
símple-mínded	/sÍmpəl máindId/	Unthinking, foolish.
spóiling for a fight	/sp⊃́iliŋ f⊃rə fáit/	Looking for trouble.

SYLLABLE (NOT-A-DIPHTHONG) & DIPHTHONG CONTRASTS: AN ENGLISH SPELLING PATTERN

QUESTION: When is a diphthong NOT a diphthong?

ANSWER: When a consonant sound appears between the 2 vowels creating 2 syllables, but the ALPHABET SYMBOL for the second syllable is missing. This occurs when

1. ALPHABET LETTERS r or l follow a diphthong, or when
2. invisible /w/ and invisibile /y/ are phonologically present between 2 vowel sounds, creating 2 syllables.

NOTE: The relationships between /r/ & /l/ and invisible /w/ & invisible /y/ are very close. When diphthongs are present, with few exceptions the presence of /r/ or /l/ signals the presence of /w/ or /y/.

1a. DIPHTHONG /ai/ + /r/ or /l/ = INVISIBLE /y/

EXAMPLES:

a. DIPHTHONG /ai/				NOT-A-DIPHTHONG			
/ai/	(V+V)			/ay/+Vowel & ALPHABET LETTERS r & l			
fight	height	wide	try	tíre	tíle	líar	ríle

VOCABULARY

rile	/ráyəl/	To make someone very angry.

1b. DIPHTHONG /au/ + /r/ or /l/ = INVISIBLE /w/

EXAMPLES:

b. DIPHTHONG /au/				NOT-A-DIPHTHONG			
/au/	(V+V)			/aw/+Vowel/ & ALPHABET LETTERS w & l			
sow	house	cloud	flout	h/óur	hówl	tówer	tówel

VOCABULARY

sow	/sau/	A female pig that has given birth.
flout	/flaut/	To challenge, to disobey, authority.
hówl	/háwəl/	To yell like a dog.
tówer	/táwUr/	A tall, narrow building.

1c. DIPHTHONG /ɔi/ + /r/ or /l/ = INVISIBLE /y/

EXAMPLES:

DIPHTHONG /ɔi/				NOT-A-DIPHTHONG			
/ɔi/	(V+V)			/ɔy/+Vowel) & ALPHABET LETTERS r & l			
joy	choice	cloy	Troy	óil	láwyer	fóyer	toil

VOCABULARY

cloy	/klɔi/	An overpowering (too strong) scent (smell).
fóyer	/fɔ́yə/	An entry hall in a house or an apartment.
tóil	/tɔ́yəl/	Very hard work.

A 2-SYLLABLE/NOT-A-DIPHTHONG /áyə/ LIMERICK

There wás a jólly young gíant,

All gréen, ten feet táll and quite plíant.

He símpered and smíled,

All the gírls thought him míld,

Till he stómped them to búrger and fríed 'em.

VOCABULARY		
jólly	/ǰáli/	To be very happy and full of fun.
plíant	/pláyInt/	To be flexible, to be easy to persuade.
símper	/sÍmpUr/	To giggle and flirt in a childish manner.
stomp	/st*a*mp/	To step on an object and crush it.

2. a. BETWEEN TWO ALPHABET VOWELS: INVISIBLE /y/

beátify meánder liabílity reáct

b. BETWEEN TWO ALPHABET VOWELS: INVISIBLE /w/

óur/hóur sóur flóur devóur

HOW TO REMAIN A DIPHTHONG: ADD ING TO THE END OF THE WORD
/r/ or /l/ + INVISIBLE /w/ or INVISIBLE /y/ + ING

INVISIBLE /y/ or /w/			DIPHTHONG + ING		
EXAMPLES:					
/áyUr/	/áwUr/	/ɔ́yəl/	/ai/	/au/	/ɔi/
flíer	hóur	bóil	flying	hówling	bóiling

NOTE: See Chapter III, pages 177–178 for further explanations and examples of INVISIBLE y.

REVIEW EXERCISES

THE DIPHTHONGS /ai/ & /au/ & /⊃i/

SPEAKING & PHONEME WRITING EXAMPLES: CONTRASTING THE DIPHTHONGS & VOWEL + ALPHABET y & w

/ai/ & /au/ & /⊃i/ /a/+y & /a/+w & /⊃/+y

1. Our hóuse has a wíde tíled fóyer.

2. A góod láwyer will fóil a góod líar.

3. I líke to hówl at the móon whén I'm ríled.

4. I'm flyíng to Chína next Fríday.

5. Flóyd's pet móuse is annóying me.

6. Hóward's been indícted. His tríal's péndíng.

7. Míles is a líar. He líes áll the tíme.

8. Hóward and Móira clímbed the Tówer of Písa last yéar.

VOCABULARY

fóil	/f⊃́yəl/	To frustrate or prevent something bad from happening.
hówl	/háwəl/	To yell like a wolf.
ríled	/ráyəld/	To be very angry.
indícted	/?Indáitld/	A legal word meaning you have to go to trial.
péndíng	/péndiŋ/	An event, like a trial, will soon occur.

REVIEW EXERCISES FOR THE 13 VOWEL & 3 DIPHTHONG PHONEMES

FIND /ɔ/ & /o/ IN THIS RHYME

Péase pórridge hot, péase pórridge cold,

Péase pórridge in the pót níne days óld.

Sóme like it hot, sóme like it cold,

Sóme like it in the pót níne days old.

VOCABULARY

péase pórridge /pízpárIǰ/ A thick stew of peas.

FIND /i/ IN THIS DOGGEREL

Sléep, báby, sléep.

Thy fáther guárds the shéep.

Thy móther shákes the dréamland trée

And fróm it fáll sweet dréams for thée.

FIND /i/ IN THIS DOGGEREL

Héarts like dóors will ópe with éase

To véry, véry líttle kéys.

Dón't fórget that twó of thése

Are "Thánk you" and "Pléase."

FIND THE VOWEL & DIPHTHONG PHONEMES IN THESE DOGGERELS

Líttle drops of wáter, líttle grains of sánd

Máke a míghty ócean, and a pléasant lánd.

Ráinbow in the wést, sáilors in distréss.

Ráinbow in the éast, sáilors at péace.

Dáffy-Down-Dílly has cóme to tówn,

In a yéllow pétticoat and a gréen gówn.

Tómmy's téars and Máry's féars

Will máke them óld befóre their yéars.

If you're nót hándsome at twénty,

Nót stróng at thírty,

Nót rích at fórty,

Nót wíse at fífty,

You most líkely néver wíll be.

FIND THE VOWEL & DIPHTHONG PHONEMES IN THESE DOGGERELS

Bírds of a féather will flóck togéther,

And só will pígs and swíne.

Ráts and míce will háve their chóice,

And só will I have míne.

My líttle Pínk,

I súppose you thínk

I cánnot do withóut you.

I'll lét you knów

Befóre I gó

How líttle I cáre abóut you.

The óld wóman stánds at the túb,

The dírty clóthes to rub, rub, rub.

But whén they're cléan, and fít to be séen,

She'll dréss like a lády and dánce on the gréen.

FIND THE VOWEL & DIPHTHONG PHONEMES IN THESE DOGGERELS

Cróss-Patch, líft the látch.

Sít by the fíre and spín.

Táke a cúp and fíll it úp,

Then cáll your néighbors ín.

Yánkee Dóodle cáme to tówn,

A-ríding on a póny.

He stúck a féather in his hát,

And cálled it Macaróni.

If wíshes were hórses,

Béggars would ríde.

If túrnips were wátches,

I'd wéar one by my síde.

FIND THE VOWEL & DIPHTHONG PHONEMES IN THESE DOGGERELS

A díller, a dóllar, a tén o'clóck schólar,
Whát makes you cóme so sóon?
You úsed to cóme at tén o'clóck
And nów you cóme at nóon.

Ríde a cock-hórse to Bánbury Cróss,
To sée a fine lády upón a whíte hórse.
Ríngs on her fíngers, and bélls on her tóes,
And shé will have músic wherével she góes.

I knów a fúnny líttle mán as quíet as a móuse.
He dóes the míschief thát is dóne in éverybódy's hóuse.
Nó one's éver séen his fáce and yét we áll agrée,
That évery pláte we bréak was crácked by Mr. Nóbody.

CHAPTER III

The 25 Consonant Phonemes

INTRODUCTION

The 6 consonant phoneme categories in this chapter are

1. APICO-ALVEOLARS	2. INTERDENTALS	3. LABIO-DENTALS
4. BI-LABIALS	5. PALATO-VELARS	6. GLOTTALS

These categories identify which part of the mouth (POINT OF ARTICULATION) is being manipulated (MANNER OF ARTICULATION) by

1. the tip, blade and back of the tongue,
2. the tongue between the teeth,
3. the upper lip biting the lower lip,
4. the actions of both lips, and
5. how the larynx's glottis (vocal cords) shape the air.

All of the above contribute to creating the 25 CONSONANT phonemes of Standard American English.

REMEMBER: The majority of American English consonants are formed in the upper 2/3 of the mouth.

Figure 29. The 25 American English Consonants.

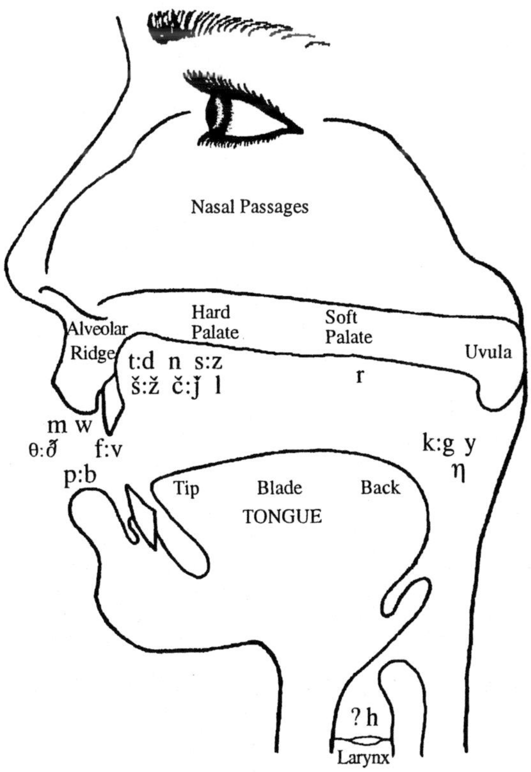

VOICED & VOICELESS CONSONANTS

VOICED means that a consonant sound is spoken aloud. The glottis vibrates. 16 OF THE 25 CONSONANT PHONEMES ARE VOICED.

4 STOPS: /b/ /d/ /g/ /ʔ/   3 NASALS: /m/ /n/ /ŋ/   1 AFFRICATE: /ǰ/

4 FRICATIVES: /v/ /z/ /ž/ /ð/   2 LIQUIDS: /r/ /l/   2 GLIDES: /w/ /y/

REMEMBER: All VOWELS and DIPHTHONGS are voiced as well.

VOICELESS means that a consonant sound is "whispered." The glottis does NOT vibrate. 9 CONSONANT PHONEMES ARE VOICELESS.

3 STOPS: /p/ /t/ /k/   1 AFFRICATE: /č/

5 FRICATIVES: /f/ /s/ /š/ /θ/ /h/

THE 6 CONSONANT CATEGORIES IN THIS CHAPTER

1. THE 10 APICO-ALVEOLAR/UPPER TEETH ROOT RIDGE CONSONANTS

2 stops	1 nasal	1 liquid
/t/ & /d/	/n/	/l/

4 fricatives	2 affricates
/s/ & /z/ /š/ & /ž/	/č/ & /ǰ/

2. THE 2 INTERDENTAL/BETWEEN-THE-TEETH FRICATIVES

2 interdentals
/θ/ & /ð/

3. THE 2 LABIO-DENTAL/UPPER TEETH:LOWER LIP FRICATIVES

2 fricatives
/f/ & /v/

4. THE 4 BI-LABIAL/TWO-LIPS CONSONANTS

2 stops	1 nasal	1 glide
/p/ & /b/	/m/	/w/

5. THE 5 PALATO-VELAR/BACK OF THE MOUTH CONSONANTS

2 stops	1 nasal	1 glide	1 liquid
/k/ & /g/	/ŋ/	/y/	/r/

6. THE 2 GLOTTAL/VOCAL CORDS CONSONANTS

1 stop	1 fricative
/ʔ/	/h/

NOTE: Liquids /l/ & /r/ are in the Palato-Velar section, pages 121–134.

THE TWO APICO-ALVEOLAR PLOSIVE STOPS /t/ & /d/

VOICELESS /t/ & VOICED /d/

Figure 30.

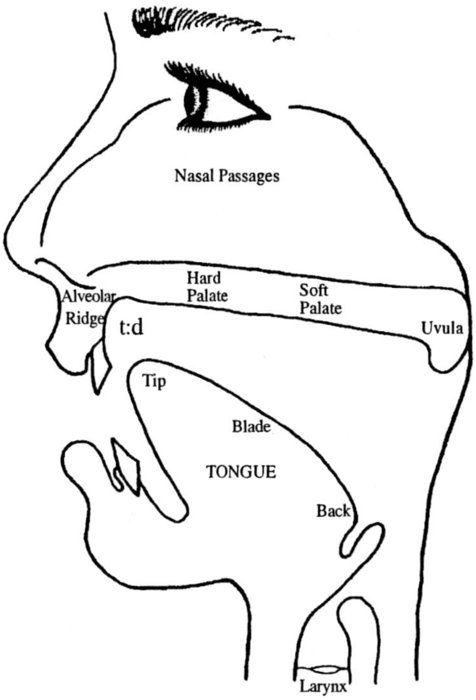

TO ARTICULATE /t/ & /d/

1. Bounce the tip of the tongue off the alveolar ridge (root ridge of the upper teeth).
2. Be sure to lift the middle and back of the tongue.

SPEAKING & PHONEME WRITING CONTRAST EXERCISES: /t/ & /d/

1. Dó dóuble your tíme, Thómas.

2. You twírl your batón divínely, Drusílla.

3. Bútton your míttens, kíttens.

4. Sit stíll untíl I finish, Dawn.

FIND /?ai/ & /t/ IN THIS RHYME

Good níght,

Sleep tíght.

Wáke up bríght

In the mórning líght.

FIND VOWEL PHONEMES IN THIS SONG

A /t/ SONG: I'M A LITTLE TEAPOT

Í'm a líttle téapot, shórt and stóut,

Hére is my hándle, hére is my spóut.

Whén I gét all stéamed up, héar me shóut.

Típ me óver and póur me óut.

VOCABULARLY

stout	/staut/	Heavy, overweight.
spout	/spaut/	The curved opening of a teapot from where you pour the tea.

A /t/ & /d/ RHYME

Twéedledée and Twéedledúm

Were twó tíny drúmmers.

Dée was táller

And Dúm was stóuter,

But bóth were éxcellent húmmers.

VOCABULARY

hum	/hʌm/	To sing with your mouth closed so that only the melody is heard.

A /t/ LIMERICK

An old flútist who tóoted and tútored,

Grew tíred of <u>mínimum</u> <u>lúcre</u>.

She tóok up her <u>túcker</u>,

And fléw to <u>Bankók</u>-er,

Where she <u>retóol</u>ed and becáme a <u>trúcker</u>.

VOCABULARY

<u>mínimum</u>	/mÍnImәm/	Very little, the least.
<u>lúcre</u>	/lúkәr/	Money.
<u>túcker</u>	/tΛ́kUr/	An Australian English word for food.
<u>Bankók</u>	/bænkά́k/	The capitol city of Thailand (Siam).
<u>retóol</u>	/ritúl/	To learn a new trade.
<u>trúcker</u>	/trΛ́kUr/	The driver of a truck.

A /t/ & /č/ RIDDLE

Hów can you téll twin wítches apárt?

You cán't tell whích witch is whích....

Unléss they are <u>fratérnal</u> twins.

VOCABULARY

<u>fratérnal</u>	/frәtÚrnәl/	Twins born of two different eggs.

A /t/ DOGGEREL

Líttle Tómmy Túcker,

Sáng for his súpper.

But áll he gót

Was brówn bréad and bútter,

FIND VOWEL PHONEMES & /t/ & /d/ IN THIS DIALOGUE

LEVEL I: A /t/ & /d/ DIALOGUE: A SEPTEMBER TUESDAY

Donna: Wéll, Thómas?

Thomas: What ís it, Dónna?

Donna: Todáy's Túesday.

Thomas: So whát?

Donna: The fírst Túesday in Septémber.

Thomas: Gét to the póint.

Donna: Remémber our déer húnting dáte upstáte?

Thomas: Drát! I forgót.

Donna: Whát do you wánt to dó abóut it?

Thomas: Gíve me tén mínutes to get réady.

Donna: You háve fiftéen.

Thomas: Gréat. Nów we wón't be láte for our húnting dáte.

FIND VOWELS, DIPHTHONGS & /t/ & /d/ PHONEMES IN THIS DIALOGUE

LEVEL II/III: A /t/ & /d/ DIALOGUE: DONNA & TINA

Donna: Tína, dón't you lóve béing twíns?

Tina: Définitely. Partícularly when our téachers can't téll us apárt.

Donna: Remémber when Mr. Dónnelly, our dráwing téacher, úsed us as módels?

Tina: So our clássmates could fíne-túne their percéptions of détails?

Donna: His expériment dídn't wórk.

Tina: Thát day we arríved dressed exáctly alíke.

Donna: And we ácted alíke that entíre hóur.

Tina: We dróve them núts!

Donna: Whát a blást!

Tina: Lét's do it agáin!

Donna: Ríght ón!

VOCABULARY

percéption	/pUrsέpšIn/	How one sees another person or an event.
expériment	/?ɛkspέrImInt/	To see if an action will work.

3 ___ed GRAMMAR AND PHONEME NOTES

ALPHABET LETTERS ___ed, the Past Tense marker of regular verbs, are pronounced 3 different ways, depending upon the kind of sound that comes before it.

1. VOICED   2. VOICELESS   or   3. /t/ & /d/.

1. When ALPHABET LETTERS ___ed follow a voiced consonant, such as b g r l m n ŋ v ð z ž ǰ or by any of the 13 vowels and 3 diphthongs (Remember? They're all voiced), then ALPHABET LETTERS ___ed are pronounced /d/.

EXAMPLES: **/___d/**

clubbed   hogged   barred   holed   timed   tanned

VOCABULARY

clubbed	/klʌbd/	To beat someone with a large, thick stick.
hógged	/hagd/	A greedy person who grabs more than its share.
barred	/bard/	To prevent or refuse admittance.

2. When the ALPHABET LETTERS ___ed follow a voiceless consonant, such as p k f θ s š č, then ALPHABET LETTERS ___ed are pronounced /t/.

EXAMPLES: **/___t/**

hopped   banked   puffed   bequéathed   tossed   mashed   blanched

VOCABULARY

puffed	/pʌft/	Blew air out of the mouth, as in blowing out a candle.
bequéathed	/bikwíθt/	To have willed money and/or property to someone.
blanched	/blænčt/	To have buried a vegetable so that it turns white.

3. But, when ALPHABET LETTERS ___ed follow /t/ & /d/, then the sounds are /___tId/ & /___dId/.

EXAMPLES: **/___tId/** **/___dId/**

wánted   ráted   ríghted   énded   sánded   clóuded

THE VOICED APICO-ALVEOLAR NASAL /n/

Figure 31.

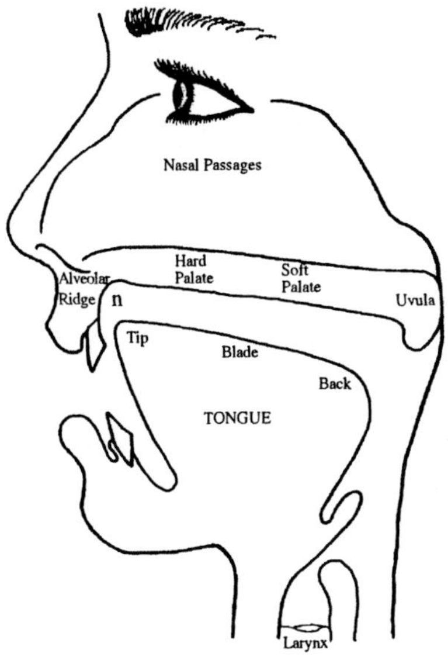

TO ARTICULATE /n/

1. Press the tip of the tongue against the alveolar ridge.
2. At the same time, close the air passage with the back of the tongue.

SPEAKING & PHONEME WRITING EXERCISES: NASAL /n/

1. Nína's a núrse on Nantúcket Island.

2. Only a nínny knócks on an ópen door.

3. No, nó, Nanétte. Nót now.

4. Néver néedle a nérvous pórcupine.

VOCABULARY

néedling/néedle	/nídliŋ/	Annoying someone.
nínny	/nÍni/	A silly, unthinking person.
nérvous	/nUrvIs/	Upset.
pórcupine	/pɔ́rkyupain/	A mammal with spines growing from its skin.

AN /n/ DOGGEREL

Cóbbler, cóbbler, ménd my shóe.

Gét it dóne by hálf-past twó.

Stítch it úp, stítch it dówn,

And thén I'll gíve you a hálf-a-crówn.

AN /n/ LIMERICK

A Nánking nánny named Náncy,

Náiled a táll man who strúck her fáncy.

She núzzled his néck.

He fléd, a tótal wréck,

While Náncy decríed his inconstáncy.

VOCABULARY

Nánking	/nǽnkíŋ/	A city in China.
nánny	/nǽni/	Someone who takes care of children.
nail	/nel/	To be able to force someone to do what you want it to do.
strúck her fancy	/strʌ́k hUr fǽnsi/	She liked him.
núzzle	/nʌ́zəl/	What a baby does when it is searching for a nipple.
fled	/flɛd/	The past tense of to fly, to escape in a hurry.
wreck	/rɛk/	A totally destroyed object. A person who is very upset.
decrý	/dicrái/	To rightly complain about a person, an action, or an event.
incónstancy	/?InkánstInsi/	Undependable. SYLLABLE STRESS here is correct.

TWO /n/ WEATHER RHYMES

Ráin befóre séven, fíne by eléven.

A súnshiney shówer won't lást hálf-an-hóur.

Réd sky at níght, shépherd's delíght.

Réd sky in the mórning, shépherd's wárning.

VOCABULARY

shépherd	/šɛ́pUrd/	Someone who protects a flock of sheep.

AN /n/ RHYME

I éat my péas with hóney,

I've dóne it áll my lífe.

It mákes the péas taste fúnny,

But it stícks them to the kníefe.

FIND THE VOWELS, DIPHTHONG /?ai/ & /n/ IN THIS DOGGEREL

Sée this prétty gírl of míne.

She bróught me hóme a pénny.

A pénny and a bóttle of wíne.

My líttle gírl can dó plénty!

AN /?em/ & /?en/ DOGGEREL

My dáme has a táme, táme cráne.

My dáme hath a cráne that's láme.

Práy, géntle Jáne,

Lét my dáme's táme cráne

Féed and thén come hóme agáin.

LEVEL I/II: AN /n/ DIALOGUE: NINO & NORMAN

Norman:	Níno. I néed your hélp. I <u>ínjure</u>d my knée.
Nino:	Nó kídding! What <u>nonsénsical</u> thíng have you dóne nów?
Norman:	Whát do you méan? I néver do nonsénsical thíngs.
Nino:	Remémber lást Súnday níght?
Norman:	All I díd was dróp my nápkin.
Nino:	Exáctly. Whén you bént down to <u>retríeve</u> it...
Norman:	Néver mind.
Nino:	You knócked óver the táble...
Norman:	I sáid never mínd!
Nino:	So whát háppened nów?
Norman:	Néver mínd.

VOCABULARY

<u>ínjure</u>	/?ÍnjUr/	To hurt or harm.
<u>nonsénsical</u>	/nansɛ́nsIkəl/	Silly or foolish.
<u>retríeve</u>	/retrív/	To rescue or pick up an object.

LEVEL II/III: AN /n/ DIALOGUE: IN A MINUTE!

Annie:	Ándrew! I néed a hánd!
Andrew:	Just a mínute, Ánnie.
Annie:	I néed you nów!
Andrew:	In a mínute!
Annie:	Ándrew! Nów! And húrry!
Andrew:	Hónestly, Ánnie, I cán't just stóp in the míddle!
Annie:	Stép on it! I cán't hold the píano up much lónger!
Andrew:	Háng on anóther sécond! Hére's the bénch!
Annie:	Plánt it únder the piáno! Thánks. What tóok you so lóng?
Andrew:	I was knéading the púmpernickel dóugh.
Annie:	Lóusy tíming, Andy.
Andrew:	I knów.

VOCABULARY

púmpernickel	/pÁmpUrnIkəl/	A dark brown bread.
dough	/do/	A mixture of flour, water, salt and yeast to bake into bread.

THE APICO-ALVEOLAR FRICATIVES /s/ & /z/

VOICELESS /s/ & VOICED /z/

Figure 32.

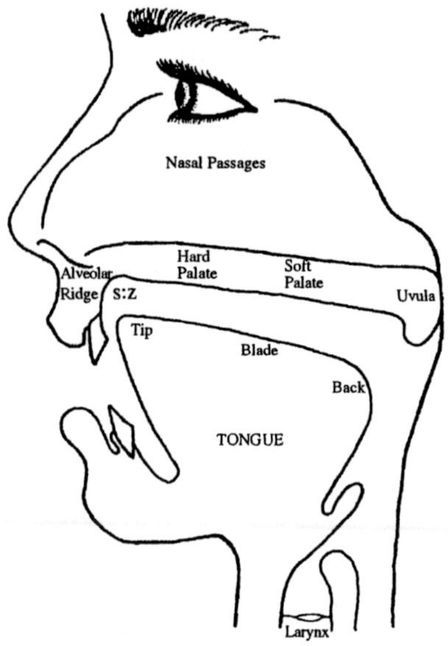

TO ARTICULATE /s/ & /z/

1. Lift the back and center of the tongue. The tip should almost touch the alveolar ridge.
2. Then hiss and squeeze the air out of your mouth.

SPEAKING & PHONEME WRITING CONTRAST EXERCISES: /s/ & /z/

1. Speak slówer, Zélda.

2. Snóopy's a sílly só-and-so.

3. Súmmer bréezes are sóft and wárm.

4. Ráiny days máke me crázy.

5. Só, súe me!

AN /s/ RHYME

Súlky Sue is ín a snit.

Súlky Sue just lóves to stew.

VOCABULARY

súlky	/sʌ́lki/	In a bad mood and enjoying it.
snit	/snIt/	Being angry at something that is really not important.
stew	/stu/	Very angry at someone.

AN /s/ RIDDLE

Two síblings are wé.

Yet thís I must sáy.

Gréat burdens we béar.

We are fúll all the dáy.

Áll day we are préssed,

But émpty when we rést.

VOCABULARY

síblings	/sÍbliŋz/	All of one's sisters and brothers.
búrden	/bÚrdIn/	A very heavy bundle or load that one must carry.

WHAT ARE WE?

A PAIR OF SHOES/BOOTS/SANDALS/SLIPPERS

AN /s/ & /z/ RHYME

Gírls and bóys, cóme out to pláy.

The móon is shíning as bríght as dáy.

Léave your súpper, léave your sléep.

And méet your pláymates óut in the stréet.

A /s/ & /š/ TONGUE TWISTER

Shé sells séashells át the séashore.

AN /s/ DOGGEREL

Símple Símon mét a píeman gǿing to the fáir

Said Símple Símon to the píeman,

"Lét me táste your wáre."

Sáid the píeman to Símple Símon,

"Shów me fírst your pénny."

Said Símple Símon to the píeman,

"Alás, I háve not ány."

VOCABULARY

alás /?əlǽs/ That's too bad.

FIND /z/ IN THIS RHYME

Whát do you suppóse?

A bée sat on my nóse.

Thén what dó you thínk?

She gáve me a wínk, and said,

"I bég your párdon.

I thóught you wére a gárden."

LEVEL I/II: AN /s/ & /z/ DIALOGUE: EXERCISE CLASS

Zachary:	Śylvia! Spéed it up!
Sylvia:	Sít on it, Záchary! I'll be réady in a sécond.
Zachary:	We're álways late for éxercise class!
Sylvia:	My zípper's stuck!
Zachary:	Slíp ínto sómething else!
Sylvia:	The zípper's stúck in the míddle!
Zachary:	Śylvia!
Sylvia:	Stárt the car. I'm álmost free.
Zachary:	It's abóut time!
Sylvia:	Zíp it, Zach, or I'll záp you with a stránd of wét spaghétti.

VOCABULARY

zap	/zæp/	To blast something or someone.
strand	/strænd/	A long piece of string or rope.

LEVEL II: AN /s/ & /z/ DIALOGUE: FLOWERS FOR SALE

Zelda:	Flówers for sale! Flówers for sale!
Izzy:	Miss, how múch are the dáisies?
Zelda:	Six dóllars a dózen.
Izzy:	And the róses?
Zelda:	Síxteen dóllars a dózen.
Izzy:	Lét me háve a dózen róses and a dózen dáisies.
Zelda:	That's twénty-two dóllars for twó dózen flówers.
Izzy:	Pléase wráp them up séparately.
Zelda:	Do you want cárds as wéll?
Izzy:	Nó thanks. Júst the flówers.
Zelda:	Thánk you! Pléase come agáin!
Izzy:	I súre will. 'Bye.

5 GRAMMAR NOTES ON ALPHABET LETTER s

1. PLURAL s 2. 3rd PERSON SINGULAR SIMPLE PRESENT TENSE s
3. POSSESSIVE s 4. PRONOUN/NOUN + BE-VERB CONTRACTIONS
5. POSSESSIVE PRONOUN s

1. PLURAL S

To pluralize a noun, add ALPHABET LETTER s to the end of the word.

The pronunciation of PLURAL s depends upon whether the word ends in a sound that is a. VOICED, b. VOICELESS, or c. a fricative sibilant.

a. VOICED phonemes include 1. all the VOWELS and DIPHTHONGS, 2. ALPHABET LETTERS w & y (Remember? At the ends of words w & y are vowel sounds and therefore, they are voiced) and 3. the VOICED consonants b d g ð v l r n m η. Then PLURAL s is pronounced /z/.

1. PLURAL s as /z/

EXAMPLES:

bugs bells beds barns girls loves bathes

blows trees fleas bábies plays blues pens

b. When PLURAL s is preceded by the voiceless consonants p t k θ f, then PLURAL s is pronounced /s/.

1. PLURAL s as /s/

EXAMPLES:

pups pets packs paths baths puffs calfs

c. The 6 fricative sibilants /s/ /z/ /š/ /ž/ /č/ & /ǰ/ change PLURAL s by adding /Iz/.

1. PLURAL s as /Iz/

/s/ /z/ /š/ /ž/ /č/ /ǰ/

/sIz/ /zIz/ /šIz/ /žIz/ /čIz/ /ǰIz/

EXAMPLES:

búses búzzes búshes garáges búnches júdges

clásses bréezes máshes colláges mátches fúdges

A /zIz/ RHYME

Móses suppóses his tóes-es are róses,

But Móses suppóses erróneously.

For nóbody's tóes-es are pósies of róses,

As Móses suppóses his tóes-es to bé.

VOCABULARY

suppóse	/səpóz/	To believe.
toes-es	/tózIz/	Toe /to/ is the singular, toes /toz/ is the correct plural. This unusual pronunciation is another example of POETIC LICENSE.
erróneous	/?Iróniyəs/	To be mistaken.
pósy	/pèzi/	A small bunch of flowers.

A /sIz/ RHYME

Thrée little ghósts-sis,

Sítting on pósts-sis,

Éating buttered tóasts-sis

Gréasing their físts-sis

Úp to their wrísts-sis.

Óh, what béast-sis!

To máke such féast-sis!

NOTE: Here, too, POETIC LICENSE is at work. The words ghósts-sis /góstsIz/, pósts-sis /póstsIz/, tóasts-sis /tóstsIz/, físts-sis /fIstsIz/, wrísts-sis /rIstsIz/, béasts-sis /bístsIz/, féasts-sis /fístsIz/ are normally pronounced: /gosts/, /posts/, /tosts/, /fIsts/, /rIsts/, /bists/ & /fists/.

2. 3rd PERSON SINGULAR s

The 3rd person singular, simple present tense behaves very much like 1. PLURAL S above. It, too, requires adding ALPHABET LETTER S to the end of a word. In this case, however, the word is a VERB.

The PHONEME patterns: VOICED, VOICELESS and sIz, zIz, šIz, žIz, čIz, ǰIz, are the same.

Subject Noun	Verb Phrase	Direct Object	Subject Pronoun	Verb Phrase	Direct Object
Míllie	runs	ónce a wéek.	She	runs	ónce a wéek.
Arthur	swims	évery day.	He	swims	évery dáy.
Everyone	needs	sleep.	One	needs	sleep.
Sam	skips	to schóol.	He	skips	to schóol.
The báby	sits	up nícely.	It	sits	up nícely.
Jack	bábies	his Pórche.	He	bábies	his Pórche.
Pénny	plays	golf.	She	plays	golf.
Joan	wátches	télevision.	She	wátches	télevision.
Léslie	garáges	all her cars.	She	garáges	áll her cárs.
Smítty	júdges	flówer shows.	He	júdges	flówer shows.

3. POSSESSIVE 's & s'

The POSSESSIVE is created by adding an APOSTROPHE (') + ALPHABET LETTER s to the end of a NOUN that appears in ADJECTIVE position in a NOUN PHRASE that indicates POSSESSION.

Nouns/adjectives of this kind keep their noun ability to be either a. singular or b. plural.

Another unusual aspect of POSSESSION is the case of c. 3rd PERSON SUBJECT PRONOUN it. This neuter pronoun does not take a POSSESSIVE APOSTROPHE. It would be too confusing. "Its" APOSTROPHE already appears in the CONTRACTION form as: It is/It's.

a. SINGULAR 's

When this special noun/adjective is singular, the APOSTROPHE PRECEDES the s. ___'s.

The PHONEME patterns: a. VOICED b. VOICELESS and c. sIz, zIz, šIz, žIz, čIz, ǰIz are unchanged.

EXAMPLES:

The cár's tíre is flát.

The gírl's hát is wét.

Míllie's house is red.

The fírefighter's face is sóoty.

b. PLURAL s'

When this special noun/adjective is plural, the APOSTROPHE FOLLOWS the s. ___s'.

The PHONEME patterns: a. VOICED b. VOICELESS and c. sIz, zIz, šIz, žIz, čIz, ǰIz are unchanged.

EXAMPLES:

The cárs' tíres are flát.

The gírls' háts are wét.

The Jónes' house is réd.

The fírefighters' fáces are sóoty.

c. 3rd PERSON SUBJECT PRONOUN it. In this special case of POSSESSION, the APOSTROPHE is absent.

EXAMPLES:

Its tíres are flát.	Its hát is wét.
Its hóuse is réd.	Its nóse is wét.

4. CONTRACTION 'S

Contractions apply to NOUN/PRONOUN + BE-VERB combinations. That means any NOUN or PRONOUN + the 3rd PERSON SIMPLE PRESENT TENSE BE-VERB.

Contractions are easy to spot when you are reading. Just look for a SUBJECT + BE-VERB combination. You will see an APOSTROPHE in front of ALPHABET LETTER s at the ends of a. NOUNS and b. PRONOUNS.

The APOSTROPHE (') replaces the the ALPHABET LETTERS i & a of IS & ARE.

a. SUBJECT NOUN + BE-VERB: is/are

FULL FORM	CONTRACTED FORM
Lúlu is véry fúnny.	Lúlu's véry fúnny.
Mr. Rógers is a nice man.	Mr. Rógers's a níce mán.
Jáne is páinting a múral.	Jáne's páinting a múral.
The gírls are léaving tóday.	The gírls're léaving todáy.
The wéather is véry mild.	The wéather's véry mild.

b. SUBJECT PRONOUN + BE-VERB: is/are/am

FULL FORM	CONTRACTED FORM
She ís a háppy pérson.	Shé's a háppy pérson.
It ís a lóvely évening.	It's a lóvely évening.
They are búying a sáilboat.	Théy're búying a sáilboat.
We are máking lots of móney.	Wé're máking lots of móney.
I am rúnning late.	I'm rúnning late.

5. 4 POSSESSIVE PRONOUNS S

These 4 POSSESSIVE PRONOUNS are a special category. Without ALPHABET LETTER s, they appear as ADJECTIVES in NOUN PHRASES.

Our hóuse is a twó-stóry colónial.

Her bóok is wét.

Their súpper is réady.

Your róses are blóoming.

But when ALPHABET LETTER s is attached to the ends of these POSSESSIVE PRONOUNS, that means they no longer belong in the SUBJECT NOUN PHRASE. Their new place is at the end of a sentence.

That twó-stóry colónial is óurs.

The wét book is hérs.

The súpper on the táble is théirs.

Those blóoming róses are yóurs.

REVIEW EXERCISES

FIND /s/ & /z/ IN THIS DOGGEREL?

Líttle Boy Blúe,

Cóme blów your hórn.

The shéep's in the méadow,

The ców's in the córn.

Whére's the líttle bóy

Who looks áfter the shéep?

Under the háystack fást asléep.

FIND /s/ & /z/ IN THIS RHYME?

Thróugh the téeth,

Pást the gúms.

Lóok out, stómach,

Hére it cómes!

THE 2 APICO-ALVEOLAR FRICATIVES: /š/ & /ž/

VOICELESS /š/ & VOICED /ž/

Figure 33.

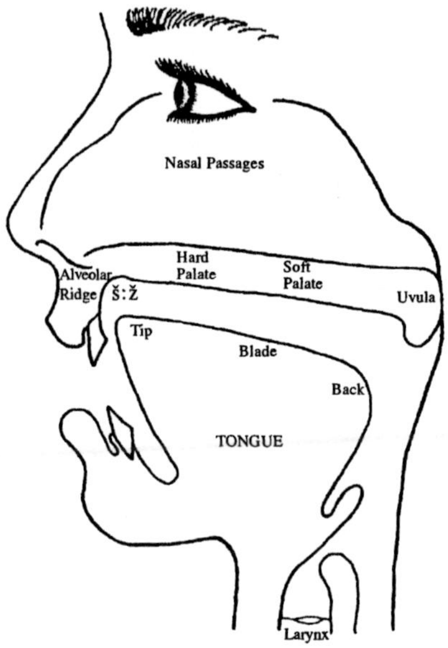

TO ARTICULATE /š/ & /ž/

1. Close your teeth.
2. Press the sides of your tongue to the inner sides of your upper molars.
3. Curl the tip of the tongue down a little.
4. At the same time, HISS! Squeeze the air out of your mouth.

NOTE: /ž/ probably entered Old English nearly a thousand years ago when the Norman French invaded Britain. Many English words come from French.

SPEAKING & PHONEME WRITING CONTRAST EXERCISES: /š/ & /ž/

1. Jéanne creátes colláges and montáges.
2. Séan's pleasure is drínking champágne.
3. Asia's ázure skies cámouflage óuter space.
4. They prédict a barráge of méteors toníght.

VOCABULARY

Jéanne	/žʌ́nə/	In French, /ǰin/ in English. The feminine of John.
colláge	/kɔlá ž/	A painting with flat pieces of paper glued on.
montáge	/mɔntá ž/	A painting with three dimensional objects glued on.
Séan	/šɔn/	In Gaelic and English. Sometimes spelled Shawn or Shaun.
champágne	/šæžpén/	A bubbly wine that originated in France.
ázure	/?ǽžUr/	A shade of sky blue. From French.
cámouflage	/kǽməflaž/	To cover an object so that it cannot be seen.
barráge	/bərá ž/	A violent rain of objects.
méteors	/mítiyUrz/	Small lumps of dirt and ice that fly in outer space.

A /š/ & /ž/ LIMERICK

<u>Gígolo</u> <u>Jean</u>'s <u>entouráge</u>,

Líve <u>en másse</u> in his garáge.

So do Shéila and Chárlotte,

Whose trúck's párked in the cár lot.

My góodness! Whát a <u>menáge</u>!

VOCABULARY

<u>gígolo</u>	/žÍgəlo/	A man who allows women to support him.
<u>Jean</u>	/zɔ̌/	French for John.
<u>entouráge</u>	/ʔ*a*ntur*á*ž/	The servants of a famous person.
<u>en másse</u>	/ʔ*a*nm*á*š/	In a group.
<u>menáge</u>	/men*á*ž/	A mixed group of people who live together.

NOTE: All of these words come from French.

A /š/ & /ž/ RHYME

Whát a pléasure to fínd such a tréasure,

A <u>profúsion</u> of Pérsian límes.

I'll <u>squísh</u> them and <u>squásh</u> them.

I'll másh them and crúsh them,

And dréam up some móre sílly rhymes.

VOCABULARY

<u>profúsion</u>	/prəfyúžIn/	A great many.
<u>squish</u>	/skwÍš/	To squeeze a spongy object, like a ripe peach.
<u>squash</u>	/skw*a*š/	To press flat a spongy object, like a ripe tomato.
<u>múlled</u>	/mΛ́ld/	Wine that has been warmed up.

FOUR /š/ & /ž/ PHONEME:SPELLING PATTERNS
IN UNSTRESSED SYLLABLES

1. ___TION = /šIn/

áction operátion fríction notátion

2. ___SION = /žIn/ or /šIn/

collísion decísion excísion ténsion séssion tórsion

NOTE: If a CONSONANT preceeds ___SION, then the sound is /šIn/. If a VOWEL preceeds ___SION, then the sound is /žIn/.

---

3. ___(S)CIOUS = /šIn/ or ___SCIENCE = /šIns/

précious cónscious cónscience

4. ___ZURE/SURE = /žUr/

ázure expósure léisure pléasure tréasure

LEVEL I/II: A /š/ & /ž/ DIALOGUE: CHARLOTTE & JEANNETTE

Charlotte: Let's sít thére, Jeanétte, in the shåde of that búsh.

Jeannette: That rúshing stréam is cóoler. And there's a trúe to shåde us.

Charlotte: We can cóol our féet in the shállows.

Jeannette: Lóok! Sáxifràge! And a tíny fúschia!

Charlotte: Let's píck some for a corságe.

Jeannette: Twó corságes. Sháre and sháre alíke.

Charlotte: Okáy. Twó corságes.

Jeannette: And a thírd corságe for líttle Sean.

Charlotte: Thrée corságes. But nó more! I'm on vacátion!

Jeannette: It's my vacátion, too!

Charlotte: So rélish it. Stop creáting work.

VOCABULARY

sáxifràge	/sáksIfræž/	A low-growing plant.
fúschia	/syúšə/	A reddish-purple flowering plant.
corságe	/k⊃sáž/	A bunch of flowers wrapped in ribbons.

LEVEL II/III: A /š/ & /ž/ DIALOGUE: SEAMUS & GERARD

Gerard: Ooooh! I'm búshed! I néed a masságe.

Seamus: Lóok at those abrásions! What háppened?

Gerard: I was húnting for tréasure.

Seamus: Gósh. You're álso súffering from expósure!

Gerard: A barráge of bóulders came túmbling dówn at me.

Seamus: And to thínk I shíed awáy from such a gréat vacátion!

Gerard: There was a míne explósion. They dídn't know I was aróund.

Seamus: So thát's how you spént your léisure! Bétter you than mé, kid!

Gerard: Oh, húsh up. Just kéep on masságing me. Ahhh. Thát feels gréat.

VOCABULARY

Séamus	/šémIs/	An Irish man's name.
masságe	/məsáž/	When someone rubs your body with its hands.
bushed	/bUšt/	Exhausted, very, very tired.
abrásions	/ʔəbréžInz/	Scraped-off skin.
treasure	/trɛ́žUr/	Gold and jewelry that has been buried.
expósure	/ʔɛkspóžUr/	Exhaustion from too much sun, rain and cold.
shied	/šaid/	Stayed away from.
explosion	/ʔɛksplóžIn/	When a bomb goes off.
leisure	/lížUr/	Free time, vacation time.

THE 2 APICO-ALVEOLAR AFFRICATES: /č/ & /ǰ/

VOICELESS /č/ & VOICED /ǰ/

Figure 34.

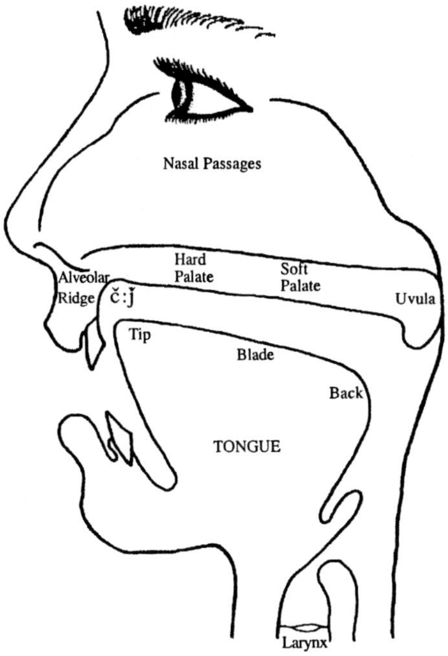

TO ARTICULATE /č/ & /ǰ/

1. Press the tip of the tongue against the alveolar ridge.
2. Then release the tip just enough to allow a little bit of air to squeeze through.

SPEAKING & PHONEME WRITING CONTRAST EXERCISES: /č/ & /ǰ/

1. Chárlie chópped two búnches of scállions.

2. I lóve chárcoal-bróiled véal chops.

3. Chípper lóves jewelry.

4. Júne is the ítchiest month.

3 /č/ & /ǰ/ CONSONANT PHONEME:SPELLING NOTES

1. In words that come from FRENCH, ch is pronounced /š/.

chartréuse chássis cháuvinism chic cachét sachét cache

VOCABULARY

chartréuse	/šartrús/	A yellow-green color.
chássis	/šæsi/	The undercarriage of a car.
cháuvinism	/šɔvInIzm/	A belief that one's country is always right.
chic	/šik/	Great style, very well dressed.
cachét	/kašé/	Having a special kind of charm.
sachét	/sæšé/	A packet of scent in your bureau drawers.
cache	/kæš/	Supplies hidden in a place that is hard to find.

2. In words that derive from GREEK, ch is pronounced /k/.

chémistry chíropracter schéme/schéma chloríne choríne

VOCABULARY

chémistry	/kɛmIstri/	A science where one mixes chemicals.
chíropracter	/káir əpræktUr/	A doctor who massages your body.
schéme/schéma	/skímə/skím/	A scheme is a plan. A schema is a drawing.
chloríne	/klɔrín/	A chemical used to remove bacteria from water.
choríne	/kɔrín/	A dancer in musical comedies of the 1920s.

3. Some GERMAN and GAELIC words with ALPHABET LETTER combination ch sound like /x/. To produce /x/ clear your throat as though you are getting ready to spit.

GERMAN		GAELIC
ach	kíchel	loch

VOCABULARY

ach	/?ax/	A German sound similar in meaning to the English "Oh!'
kíchel	/kÍxəl/	Small rolled cookies filled with nuts and jam.
loch	/lɔx/	A Gaelic word meaning lake.

A /ǰ/ DOGGEREL

Jáck and Jíll climbed úp the híll

To fétch a páil of wáter.

Jáck fell dówn and bróke his crówn,

And Jíll came túmbling áfter.

VOCABULARY

fetch	/fɛč/	To get, or bring.
crown	/kraun/	The top of one's head.
túmble	/tÁmbəl/	To fall and roll.

A /č/ RHYME

Chíp, chúnk, Chárlie, chíppety chóo

Chów down, Chárlie, chéw, chéw chéw.

A /ǰ/ DOGGEREL

Jáck, be nímble! Jáck be quíck!

Jáck! Júmp óver the cándlestick!

A /č/ FOLKSONG RIDDLE

I GAVE MY LOVE A CHERRY

I gáve my lóve a chérry that hád nó stóne.

I gáve my lóve a chícken withóut nó bóne.

I tóld my lóve a stóry that hás nó énd.

I gáve my lóve a báby with nó cryín'.

A chérry when it's blóomin' it hás no stóne.

A chícken when it's píppin' it hás no bóne.

The stóry that I lóve you will háve no énd.

A báby when it's sléepin' has nó cryín'.

A /ǰ/ RHYME

There wás a líttle gérbil

That was álways on the júmp.

It gíbbered and jábbered

'Cause it gót a gíant búmp.

VOCABULARY

gérbil	/ǰÚrbəl/	A hamster. A small rodent from Mexico.
gíbber	/ǰÍbUr/	To make noises instead of speaking.
jábber	/ǰǽbur/	To talk so fast that you cannot be understood.

A /č/ & /ǰ/ LIMERICK

A potáto chip was réading the Í Ching

While súnning hersélf at the beach-ing.

Súddenly, she héard a wild scréeching!

She júmped up, her héart a-twítching!

And for good réason! A blúe whale was béaching!

VOCABULARY

Í Ching	/?íčíŋ/	A fortune-telling Chinese book.
béach	/bič/	The seashore.
scréech	/skrič/	A loud, high-pitched scream.
twitch	/twIč/	Jerking and twisting.
blúe whale	/bl̩ú wel/	The largest whale growing to about 140 feet long.
béaching	/bíčiŋ/	When a boat or large sea animal comes up on the sand.

LEVEL I: A /č/ DIALOGUE: CHESTER & MITCHELL

Chester: Mítchell! Lóng time no sée! Lét's have lúnch.

Mitchell: Chéster! What a chámpion idéa! Next wéek?

Chester: Túesday, March 1st. Two p.m. At the Bewítched Pítcher.

Mitchell: The Bewítched Pítcher?

Chester: It's a chárming place, <u>old chum</u>. <u>Véry in</u>.

Mitchell: Is it chéap?

Chester: It's nót cheap!

Mitchell: Let's chéck out Chárlie's, instéad.

Chester: That fríed chícken réstaurant?

Mitchell: It's chéap.

Chester: It's a dáte. Sée you there.

VOCABULARY

<u>óld chúm</u>	/ʔóld čʌm/	A British English phrase for old friend.
<u>véry in</u>	/vɛ́ri yIn/	Fashionable.

LEVEL II/III: A /č/ & /ǰ/ DIALOGUE: ANGELINA & JOJO

Angelina: Jójo! Guess whát! I'm a júdge's clerk!

Jojo: That's great, Angelína! Which jústice?

Angelina: Júdge Jánice J. Júdson, of the Supréme Court!

Jojo: Whát a jób!

Angelina: Héy! Its my achíevement! I réached for it!

Jojo: You have a góod chance of becóming a júdge yoursélf someday!

Angelina: If I can stómach the pólitics.

Jojo: Yóu'll adjust.

Angelina: At thís júncture I máy as wéll enjóy my succéss.

Jojo: Cút the chítchat. Phóne the fámily. They'll chéer for yóu.

Angelina: Okay. And thánks for the suppórt.

VOCABULARY

júncture	/ǰΛ́ŋkčUr/	At this point in one's life.
chítchat	/čItčæt/	Casual, friendly talk.

Figure 35.

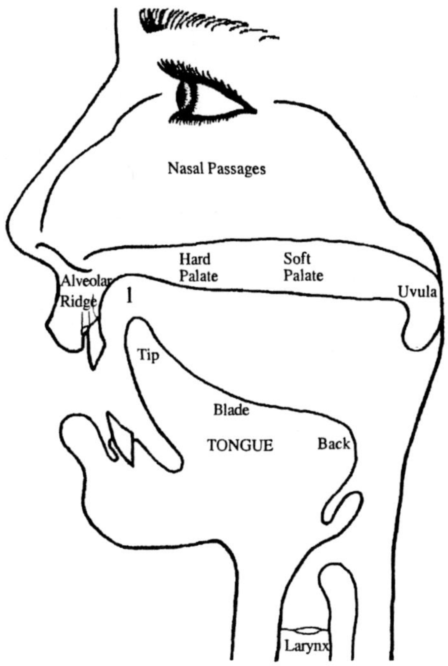

TO ARTICULATE /l/

1. Curl the tongue up and back to the roof of the mouth.

SPEAKING & PHONEME WRITING EXERCISES: /l/

1. Líght the lámp, Lúlu.
2. Whát a lóvely béach blánket.
3. The English call élevators lífts.
4. Lílly's lístening to Lárry pláy the piáno.

AN /l/ DOGGEREL

Old King Cóle was a mérry old sóul

And a mérry old sóul was hé.

He cálled for his pípe

And he cálled for his bówl,

And he cálled for his fíddlers thrée.

AN /l/ RHYME

Líttle Lúcy Láwler, síts in the párlor,

Wátching all the ládies, láughing in the árbor.

VOCABULARY

párlor /párlUr/ A living room used only when company arrives.

AN /l/ LIMERICK

There wás a young lády of Lynn

Who lóved a young lád náme of Flynn.

When she tríed to wéd him,

He replíed "Nót on your lífe, Lynn!"

So she hogtíed him, and thén she allíed him.

VOCABULARY

lad	/læd/	A young man. A male teenager.
wed	/wɛd/	To marry.
hógtíe	/hágtái/	Tying up a pig just before you slaughter it.
ally	/?ælai/	To join or marry.

AN /l/ RIDDLE

What do élephants, ócelots, cámels and áirplanes have in common?

All share the LETTER l.

VOCABULARY

ócelots /?ásəlats/ A small Central & South American spotted cat.

SYLLABIC /ə l/

When ALPHABET VOWELS a e i o u or a VOWEL PHONEME appear before /l/ in an UNACCENTED syllable, the vowel is nearly always SCHWA /ə/.

Unstressed /ə/ + /l/ occurs because in English /l/ curls up towards the alveolar ridge. This muscular action causes the tongue to bend in the middle of the mouth where SCHWA /ə/ is located.

Figure 36. SYLLABIC / ə l/ occurs in unstressed syllables at the
1. beginnings 2. middles & 3. ends of words.

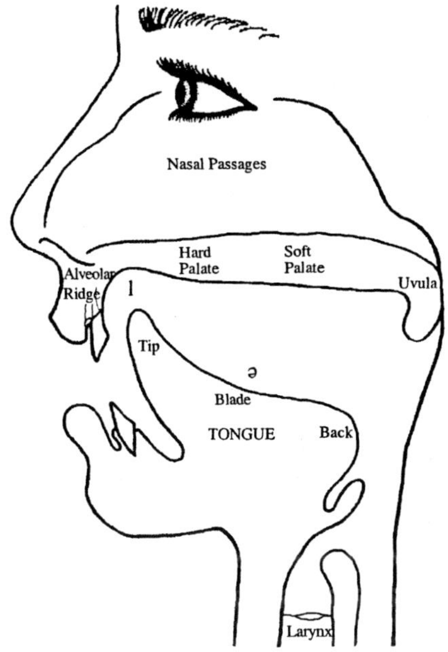

1. AT THE BEGINNINGS OF WORDS: /əl___/

allów ellípsis alíke alóne alíve

2. IN THE MIDDLE OF WORDS: /___əl___/

colléction òpaléscent àbsolútely búbbling

VOCABULARY		
opalescent	/?opəlɛsInt/	Glowing like an opal.

3. AT THE ENDS OF WORDS: /___əl/

cáble quárrel stúmble twíddle lábel

NOTE: The relationship between SCHWA /ə/ and LIQUID /l/ is a close one. See Chapter II, page 51 for a few examples.

Lily: Lúke! It's láte. You'll míss your cár pool.

Luke: Dón't béllow. I'm álmost réady.

Lily: I'm álso late. Lét's léave right awáy.

Luke: Lísten. Is thát the dóorbell?

Lily: Yés. Lét's léave.

Luke: Lénd me a hánd. I cán't fínd my cúfflinks.

Lily: Nó time to lóok for them nów. Róll up your sléeves instéad.

Luke: Lísten, Líly. We're láte évery morning!

Lily: So lét's sét the alárm fífteen mínutes éarlier!

Luke: A lóvely idea. But right now, lét's go!

Lily: Áll ríght, alréady!

VOCABULARY

cúfflinks /kʌ́fliŋks/ A set of pins for shirtsleeve cuffs that have holes instead of buttons.

LEVEL I/II: AN /l/ DIALOGUE: LUNCH BY THE LAKE?

Elizabeth: Álan! Let's gó! It's gétting láte!

Alan: Slów dówn, Líz. It's nót éven eléven.

Elizabeth: Lét's <u>hústle</u>! Todáy's Súnday. The láke will be fúll of bóats.

Alan: Will Péarl méet us at the láke?

Elizabeth: Shé and Mílton will be thére with their <u>káyak</u>.

Alan: Would I lóve to try óut their káyak!

Elizabeth: Álan, you cán't swím! Léarn to swím, first.

Alan: Okáy. Téach me.

Elizabeth: Nów?

Alan: Súre. Lét's gó to the póol instéad.

Elizabeth: You knów, Alan, sómetimes you cóme up with a réally góod idéa.

Alan: That's mé! Boy genius!

VOCABULARY

<u>hústle</u>	/hʌ́səl/	Hurry up.
<u>káyak</u>	/káyæk/	A small one-person boat. The Eskimos invented it.

LEVEL II/III: AN /l/ DIALOGUE: LAWYERS IN LOVE

Larry: Let's elópe, Léslie. Let's léave toníght.

Leslie: Lárry, we cán't elópe toníght. We're bóth in litigátion.

Larry: Our cólleagues can táke óver our clíents' cáses.

Leslie: Thát would be inexcúsable, Lárry!

Larry: If we were íll, ít would be excúsable.

Leslie: But Lárry, we're nót ill.

Larry: Yés, we áre, Léslie. We're lóve-sick.

Leslie: Lísten, my lóve. We'll elópe áfter our clíents wín their cáses.

Larry: Elóping nów is múch more romántic.

Leslie: I knów, but it's nót respónsible.

Larry: You wín. Wé'll be príncipled láwyers and deláy our flíght.

Leslie: Now lét's get báck to búsiness.

VOCABULARY

litigátion	/lItIgéšIn/	A legal term meaning to be in court.
cólleagues	/cáligz/	Fellow workers.
príncipled	/prÍncIpəld/	To be honorable.

THE VOICED PALATO-VELAR LIQUID /r/

/r/ is the most TENSE, the most muscular sound in English.

TO ARTICULATE /r/

1. Raise the blade of the tongue up to the hard palate.
2. Press the sides of the tongue hard against the inside surfaces of the upper molars.
3. Curl the tip of the tongue to the roof of the mouth.

Figure 37.

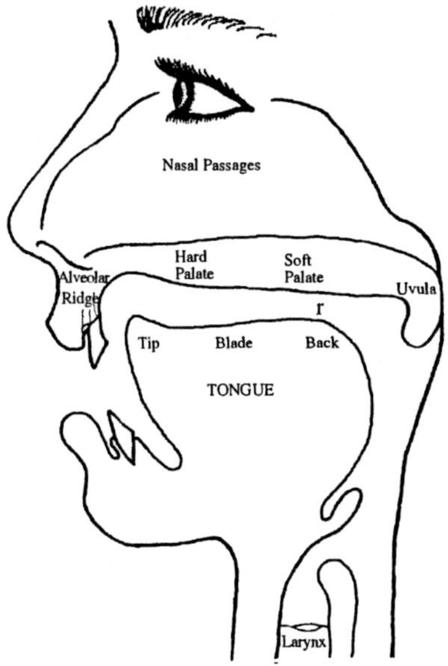

SPEAKING & PHONEME WRITING EXERCISES: /r/

1. I <u>detést</u> súmmer réruns.
2. Stráwberries are rích in mínerals.
3. Rúbber trees grów in trópical régions.
4. The Réd Ríver runs <u>rápid</u>ly in the spríng.

VOCABULARY

<u>detést</u>	/ditέst/	To dislike something or someone intensely (very much).
<u>rápid</u>	/rǽpId/	Running very fast.

A /r/ ROUND

Rów, rów, rów your bóat,

Géntly dówn the stréam.

Mérrily, mérrily, mérrily, mérrily,

Lífe is bút a dréam.

AN /r/ LIMERICK

The stráwberry's a véry sweet bérry.

It's bríght red, and it mákes réal great jélly.

But the séeds in your téeth

Can your témper make séethe.

But it's wórth it. Its táste is quíte héavenly.

VOCABULARY

seethe	/sið/	To be very angry and not be allowed to let it show.

AN /r/ RIDDLE

Hígher than a hóuse, Hígher than a trée. Whatéver can it bé?

A STAR

ANOTHER /r/ RIDDLE

Róund and róund the rúgged rock

The rágged ráscal rán.

Hów many R's are thére in thát?

Now téll me if you cán.

NONE: There is no r in THAT

VOCABULARY

rúgged	/rʌ́gId/	Rough and unfinished.
rágged	/rǽgId/	Torn clothing.
ráscal	/rǽskəl/	An unreliable person. A thief.

A THIRD /r/ RIDDLE

It's in the róck, but nót in the stóne.

It's in the márrow, but not in the bóne.

It's in the bólster, but not in the béd.

It's nót in the líving, nor yét in the déad.

What is it?

ALPHABET LETTER r

VOCABULARY

márrow	/mǽro/	The soft, not-yet-bone that you suck from a bone.
bólster	/bólstUr/	A long, hard pillow.

LEVEL I: AN /r/ DIALOGUE: RUNNING FOR THE TRAIN

Roger: Why are you rúnning, Rónnie?

Ronnie: I'm rúnning for the fóur o'cóck tráin.

Roger: Are you súre you wánt to rún for it todáy?

Ronnie: Of cóurse! I've gót to gét to wórk.

Roger: You néedn't húrry, Rónnie. Todáy's Sáturday.

Ronnie: Ráts!

LEVEL I/II: AN /r/ & /l/ DIALOGUE: LEARNING A TRADE

Ally:	Ári! Guess whát! I've gót a jób with the télephone cómpany.
Ari:	Gréat! What kínd of wórk will yóu be dóing?
Ally:	I'll be a línepérson.
Ari:	Clárify, pléase.
Ally:	I will be clímbing the télephone póles and chécking the línes.
Ari:	Are you súre you can hándle the jób?
Ally:	Of cóurse! They'll be tráining me.
Ari:	But you're no lónger in shápe.
Ally:	I've alréady begún a tráining prógram at the lócal gym.
Ari:	My! You áre sérious, áren't you?
Ally:	I súre am. And I knów I'll do wéll.
Ari:	I knów you will, tóo. Good lúck.
Ally:	Thánks.

LEVEL II/III: AN /l/ & /r/ DIALOGUE: TO QUARREL OR NOT TO QUARREL

Arlo: Márla, I'm bóred. Lét's quárrel.

Marla: Is that áll you can thínk of dóing? Gét a lífe!

Arlo: Ráin, ráin, ráin, ráin. If we dón't dó sómething sóon, I'll scréam!

Marla: Cálm dówn, Arlo. There's lóts to dó. The básement needs cléaning.

Arlo: Nó wórk.

Marla: Lísten. Sómething or sómeone is scrátching at the dóor.

Arlo: I dón't héar ánything.

Marla: Whát is it? A raccóon? A déer? A squírrel?

Arlo: Lóok, Márla! It's júst a páir of cárdinals pécking at some crúmbs!

Marla: Whát a relíef! I thóught there were róbbers at the dóor.

VOCABULARY

raccóon	/rækún/	A dog-size animal that look like it's wearing a black mask.
squirrel	/sqwÚrəl/	A small, grey animal with a bushy tail.
cardinal	/k*á*rdInəl/	A bird. The male is covered with bright red feathers.
róbbers	/r*á*bUrz/	People who steal.

SYLLABIC /r/

There are 3 SYLLABIC /r/

1. /er/ 2. /ur/ 3. /Ur/

The normal sounds of /e/ & /u/ & /U/ are truncated (shortened and tensed).

Figure 38. /er/.

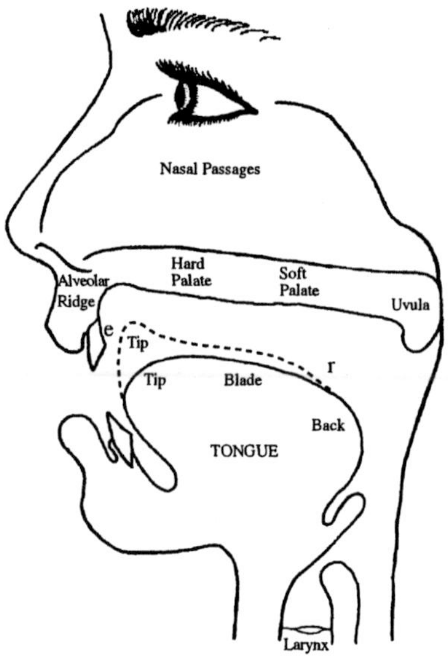

Figure 39. /ur/.

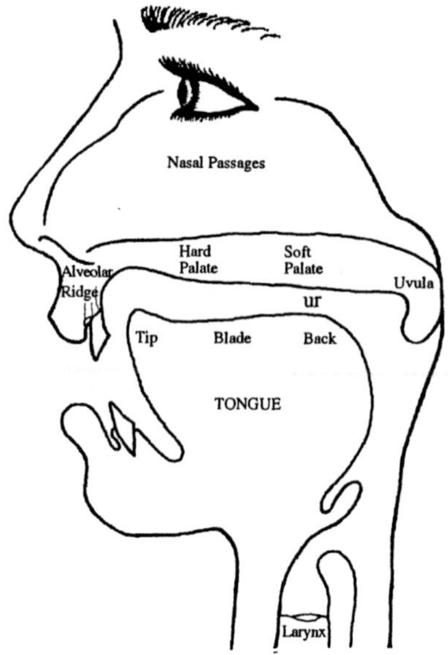

1. The /e/ + /r/ combination is the most unusual because the high tail end of /e/ is blocked. This is because, as the tongue rises back and up to produce /r/, /e/ is swallowed by /r/.

Figure 40. /Ur/.

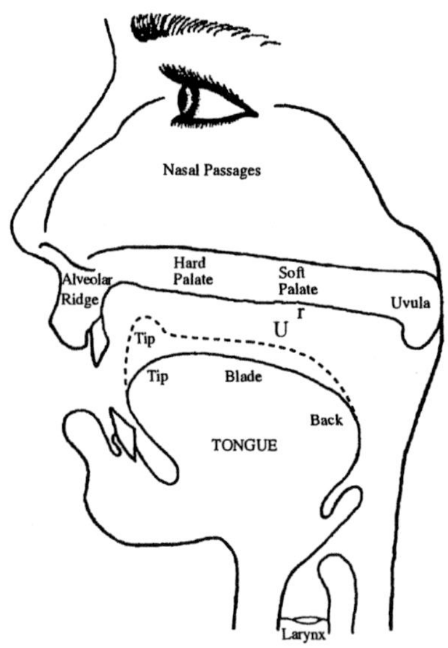

PHONEME:SPELLING NOTES ON SYLLABIC /r/

1. SYLLABIC /er/

heir/air hair/hare bare/bear

Máry flare/flair

VOCABULARY

heir	/?er/	A male who inherits property. The female form is heiress /?ɛ́rIs/.
hare	/?er/	A rabbit with very long ears and a thin body.
bare	/ber/	To be naked or empty.
bear	/ber/	A large animal that hibernates /háibUrnets/. Sleeps in winter.
flare	/fler/	A gun that shoots a bright light. Someone is in trouble.
flair	/fler/	Having a sense of style.

2. SYLLABIC /ur/

a. One SYLLABIC /ur/ category can only be pronounced

/__ur/ or /__yur/

tour poor boor dour secúre fúry immúre púrify

VOCABULARY		
boor	/bur/	Someone who is rude and insensitive.
dour	/dur/	A Scottish Gaelic word for unhappy and unpleasant.
immúre	/?Imyúr/	To bury someone while it is still alive.
púrify	/pyúrifai/	Cleanliness for religious reasons.

b. In another SYLLABIC /ur/ the words can be pronounced both as /ur/ or as /yur/.

EITHER PRONUNCIATION IS CORRECT.

/__ur/ & /__yur/

allúre lúrid adjúre dúring insúre néuron

/ur/

&

/yur/

3. SYLLABIC /Ur/

This syllabic /r/ has the most variations in spelling. It is pronounced /Ur/ in both stressed and unstressed syllables.

earn/urn were girl word world curl múrder

stern firm cértain cúrtain fúrther

VOCABULARY		
urn	/?Urn/	A large, clay pot for the bones & ashes of the dead.

SPEAKING & PHONEME WRITING CONTRAST EXERCISES: /er/ & /ur/ & /Ur/

1. Máry's hair is so cúrly!
2. Whére are the cúrtains I púrchased éarlier?
3. The póor bear lost áll its háir.
4. Are you cértain that Máry's death was múrder?
5. You're wéaring that fúr to the théater?

FIND SYLLABIC /r/ IN THESE DOGGERELS

I lóst my máre in Líncoln Láne.

I'll néver fínd her thére agáin.

Góosey, góosey, gánder,

Whíther shall I wánder?

Upstairs and dównstairs

And ín my lády's chámber.

THE TWO INTER-DENTAL FRICATIVES: /θ/ & /ð/

VOICELESS Greek theta /θ/ & VOICED Old English eth /ð/
for
ALPHABET LETTERS th

Figure 41.

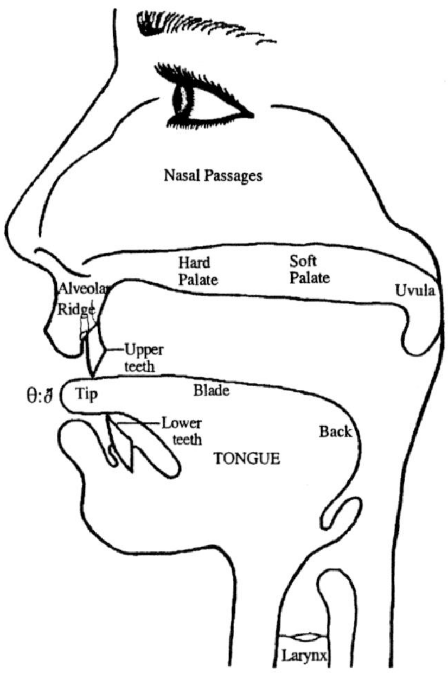

TO ARTICULATE /θ/

1. Stick out your tongue.
2. Then bite the tip gently and
3. Hiss (squeeze out a little air).

NOTE: Most ALPHABET th combinations are voiceless /θ/ (Greek theta).

SPEAKING & PHONEME WRITING CONTRAST EXERCISES: Greek /θ/ & Old English /ð/

1. Stóp <u>díthering</u>, Thélma.
2. <u>Théspian</u>s ténd to thínk theátrically.
3. "<u>Botherátion</u>!" críed the óther brother.
4. Báthing is such a <u>blíthering</u> <u>bóther</u>!

VOCABULARY

<u>díther</u>	/dÍðUr/	Making a great fuss.
<u>théspian</u>	/θέspiyIn/	A word from Greek meaning actor.
<u>botherátion</u>	/baðUréšIn/	An exclamation for Oh, my goodness!
<u>blíthering</u>	/blÍðUriŋ/	Unstoppable speech.
<u>bóther</u>	/báðUr/	Trouble. Annoy.

A /θ/ RHYME

A thíef típtoed through Thélma's théatre,

Stéaling a thérmos and a tíny wáter héater.

We thóught and thóught why this hóld-up mán

Ignóred her gold Góthic wédding band.

VOCABULARY

thief	/θif/	Someone who steals.
thérmos	/θÚrmIs/	A container that keeps liquids hot or cold.
Góthic	/gáθIk/	A group of ancient (old-time) German tribes.

AN /ð/ RHYME

Thís, thát, thém, thóse,

Théir/thére, whíther/wíther,

Móther, fáther, síster, bróther,

I thínk these eths are a blíthering bóther.

VOCABULARY

whíther	/hwÍðUr/	An archaic (old) way of asking where?
wíther	/wÍðUr/	To dry up.
eth	/ʔɛð/	The Old English symbol for ALPHABET LETTERS th

/θ/ & /ð/ PHONEME:SPELLING NOTE

THE DEFINITE ARTICLE the

DEFINITE ARTICLE the has 2 pronunciations:

1. When the comes before words that begin with a consonant sound, it is pronounced /ðə/.

   a. The sún's shíning.

   b. Clóse the wíndow.

   c. Whére's the bús stop?

   d. I háve the kéys.

2. When the comes before words that begin with ALPHABET VOWELS, then the is pronounced /ði/.

   The pattern is /_i/ + /y/ + a vowel phoneme.
   /y/ replaces the GLOTTAL STOP /ʔ/.

NOTE: All words that begin with an ALPHABET VOWEL a e i o u can only be articulated by contracting the vocal cords. Vowels cannot be heard or produced unless they "consonantalized" or voiced. The GLOTTAL STOP /ʔ/ is the only English phoneme without its own alphabet letter. /ʔ/ is the only English consonant that is heard, but never seen. See Chapter III, pages 181–182 for more detailed explanations of /ʔ/ to /y/ pronunciation patterns.

---

a. The ápple is rípe.

ðiyǽpəlIzráip

b. Pút the óil on the táble.

pÚt ðiyɔ́yəlan ðətébəl

c. The óven's hót.

ðiyʌ́vInz hát

d. Bóil the égg for twó mínutes.

bɔ́yəlðiyɛ́g fɔr tú mÍnIts

LEVEL I/II: A /θ/ & /ð/ DIALOGUE: BETH & THEODORE

Beth:	Théodore, is thís the thímble you lóst?
Theo:	Thánks, Beth. I thóught it was stólen.
Beth:	Its wálls are thíck. Sílver?
Theo:	Yép. I've thírteen more.
Beth:	Wów! They múst be wórth a lót.
Theo:	I'm nót wéalthy, but thís colléction is spécial.
Beth:	How cóme?
Theo:	Théy're Thessálian. Thrée-thóusand-yéar-old Greek thímbles.
Beth:	Now thát's sómething!
Theo:	You bét. Would you líke to sée the rést of thém?
Beth:	Súre. Hów abóut next Thúrsday?
Theo:	Sée you thén.

VOCABULARY

thimble /θÍmbəl/ A sewing tool that protects a finger from a needle.

LEVEL II/III: A /θ/ & /ð/ DIALOGUE: THROUGH THICK & THIN

Ethel: Séth! Móther and fáther are míssing!

Seth: That's térrible!

Ethel: There's nó word.

Seth: It's unthínkable that théy may be . . .

Ethel: Lét's táble that thóught. We've béen through wórse.

Seth: Like the tíme those thíeves bróke ínto the hóuse?

Ethel: We thóught they'd shóot us!

Seth: Mom and Dad stýmied their gúns.

Ethel: They súre did!

Seth: Móther preténded to fáint.

VOCABULARY

through thíck and thín	/θru θÍkænd θIn/	We help each other out, in good times and in bad.
lét's táble	/lɛts tébəl/	We'll discuss the problem later.
stymie	/stáimi/	To prevent.
faint	/fent/	To fall down unconscious.

Ethel: One of the thíeves drópped his gún and tríed to cátch her.

Seth: Then Móm grábbed his thróat and thróttled him.

Ethel: Thát áction distrácted the óther two.

Seth: Dád júmped the sécond thug.

Ethel: And yóu and I attácked the thírd one and thráshed him.

Seth: Whát a thríll that was! Thínk they'll be okáy?

Ethel: Sóoner or láter the authórities will lét us knów.

Seth: I hópe the néws will be góod news.

Ethel: I thínk they will be áll right.

VOCABULARY

throttle	/θrát əl/	To choke someone.
distract	/dIstrǽkt/	To change the subject.
thug	/θΛg/	A thief who also hits people.
thrash	/θræš/	To beat very hard.
thrill	/θrIl/	A very exciting feeling.
authorities	/?⊃θárItiz/	The police, the government.

THE FOUR LABIALS OR LIP CONSONANTS: /p/ & /b/ & /m/ & /w/

VOICELESS /p/ & VOICED /b/ are PLOSIVES: STOPS that explode.

VOICED /m/ is a BI-LABLIAL NASAL. VOICED /w/ is a BI-LABIAL GLIDE.

Figure 42.

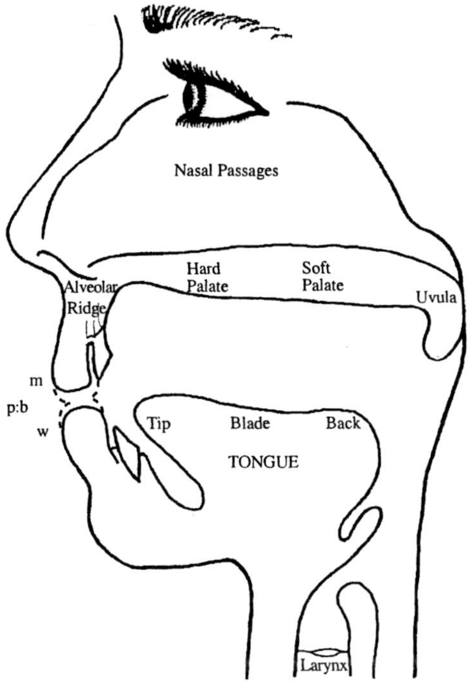

Figure 43.

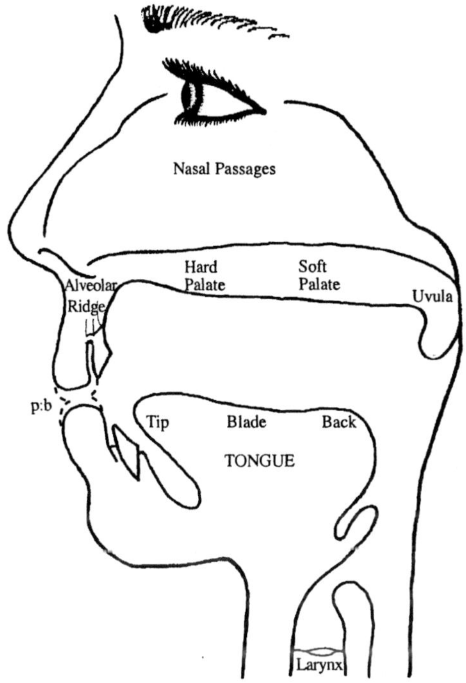

TO ARTICULATE VOICELESS /p/ & VOICED /b/

1. Put your lips together & stop the air.
2. Then puff it out of your mouth.

SPEAKING & PHONEME WRITING CONTRAST EXERCISES: /p/ & /b/

1. Pléase be <u>depéndable</u>, Bóbby.

2. Péter's abílity to <u>bambóozle</u> me is blúnted.

3. Belínda has a beaútiful báby bóy.

4. The rábbit hópped and the cráb grábbed.

VOCABULARY

<u>depéndable</u>	/dipέndəbəl/	To be helpful.
<u>bambóozle</u>	/bæmbúzəl/	To try and fool someone.
<u>blúnted</u>	/blʌ́ntId/	Ineffective.

A /p/ DOGGEREL

Péter, Péter, púmpkin-éater

Hád a wífe, but cóuldn't kéep her.

He pút her in a púmpkin shéll

And thére he képt her véry well.

VOCABULARY

púmpkin	/pʌ́mpkIn/	A large, round orange squash.
púmpkin-eater	/pʌ́mpkInítUr/	A country person.
púmpkin shell	/pʌ́mpkIn šɛl/	A house in the country.

A /p/ TONGUE-TWISTER

Péter Píper pícked a péck of píckled péppers.

A péck of píckled péppers Péter Píper pícked.

A /b/ LIMERICK

A bónnie blúebottle buzzed búsily,

From flówer to flówer, quite dízzily.

Búmping ínto a bée,

She excláimed, "Oh, párdon me!"

Who then stúng it till its fúr was all frízzily.

VOCABULARY

blúebottle	/blúbatəl/	A horsefly.
frízzy	/frÍzi/	When one's hair curls and stands up in damp weather.

A /b/ TONGUE-TWISTER

I

Bétty Bótter bóught some bútter.

"Bút," she sáid, "The bútter's <u>bítter</u>.

If I pút it ín my <u>bátter</u>,

It will máke my bátter bítter."

Bút a bít of bétter bútter

Will súrely máke my bátter bétter."

II

Só, she bóught a bít of bútter,

Bétter thán her bítter bútter.

Thén she pút it ín her bátter,

And the bátter wasn't bítter.

So, 'twas bétter Bétty Bótter

Bóught that bít of bétter bútter.

VOCABULARY

<u>bátter</u>	/bútUr/	A mixture of flour, milk, and eggs for pancakes.
<u>bítter</u>	/bǽtUr/	A sharp, unpleasant flavor.

A /p/ DOGGEREL

Fíve líttle péas in a péapod préssed.

One gréw, two gréw, and só did áll the rést.

They gréw and gréw, and they díd not stóp,

'Tíl áll of a súdden, the pód went POP!

ANOTHER /p/ DOGGEREL

Géorgie Pórgie, púdding and píe,

Kíssed the gírls and máde them cry.

Whén the bóys came óut to pláy,

Géorgie Pórgie rán awáy.

A THIRD /p/ DOGGEREL

Pússycat, pússycat, whére have you béen?

"I've béen to Lóndon to sée the quéen."

Pússycat, pússycat, whát did you thére?

"I fríghtened a líttle móuse únder her cháir."

LEVEL I/II: A /p/ & /b/ DIALOGUE: PEONIE & BOBBY

Bobby: Phéw! Am I póoped!

Peonie: Póunding pósts on the práirie, báby bróther?

Bobby: Pléase put your fúnny bone báck in your púrse. I'm tóo beat to appréciate your brílliant buffóonery.

Peonie: Wríting a térm páper for Polítical Scíence the níght befóre it's dúe is nót too bríght.

Bobby: Beaútifully put. Now béat it so I can gét some slúmber.

Peonie: Bye, bye, báby.

Bobby: Out!

VOCABULARY

póoped	/púpt/	Exhausted. Very, very tired.
póunding pósts on the práirie	/páunding póstsan ðə préri/	Working very hard. The prairie is another name for the western U.S. grasslands. To keep the cattle from wandering you have to dig holes and hammer in the thick wooden posts that hold the barbed wire fences.
fúnny bone	/fʌ́nibon/	The oléocranun /?olɛ́krənən/ process. The elbow joint which hurts when you hit it. But also makes you laugh.
buffóon	/bʌfún/	A silly clown.
béat it	/bítIt/	Go away!
slúmber	/slʌ́mbUr/	A deep, peaceful sleep.

LEVEL II/III: A /p/ & /b/ DIALOGUE: PRISCILLA & BELINDA

Belinda: Príssy, pléase put the ápple pie in the pántry.

Priscilla: Pút it there yoursélf. I'm búsy with the néw púppies.

Belinda: Did Prunélla give bírth alréady?

Priscilla: This p.m. Three bóys and two gírls.

Belinda: Oóoh! What beaútiful bábies!

Priscilla: Píebald like their pápa, Brían.

Belinda: Excépt for thís púppy. She's áll brown.

Priscilla: Only her páws are a pále beige.

Belinda: Do we háve to put them áll up for sále?

Priscilla: We'll éach choose óne púppy. But the rést múst be sóld.

Belinda: It's só hard to píck just óne. They're áll so cúte!

VOCABULARY

pántry	/pǽntri/	A closet or room for storing canned good and other food.
píebald	/páibɔld/	Different colors in large spots.
beige	/bež/	A French word for a very light brown color.

Figure 44.

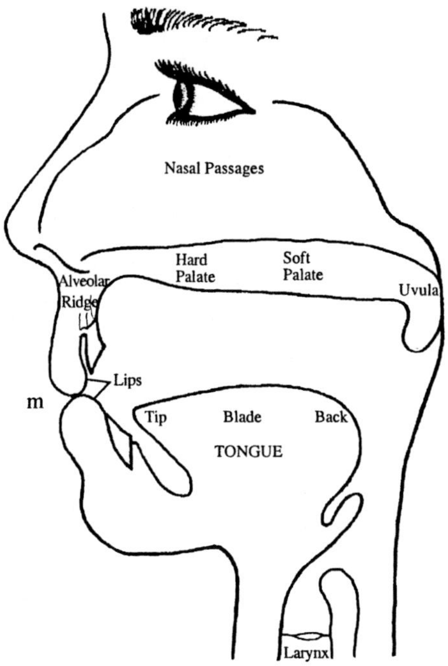

TO ARTICULATE /m/

1. Press your lips together. Hum.
2. Let the air seep out of your nose.
3. Press the back of the tongue down so that it closes the air passage.

SPEAKING & PHONEME WRITING EXERCISES: /m/

1. My móther makes márvelous marmaláde.
2. Mínnie Mouse is a fémale.
3. Clímb that límb, Símon.
4. The hámper clamp is jámmed.

VOCABULARY

marmaláde	/mɑrməléd/	A sweet jelly made of sugar and orange peel.
límb	/lIm/	A large tree-branch.
hámper	/hǽmpUr/	A box for holding laundry or food for a picnic.
clamp	/klǽmp/	The hook that closes a box.
jámmed	/ǰǽmd/	To be stuck, unmoving.

AN /m/ RHYME

Máry Mártin míxes mústard

In a míxing bówl.

Máry's mix is so spícy,

It mákes my nóse run cóld.

AN /m/ LIMERICK

A máiden of the MúMu nátion,

A módel of civilizátion,

Was mílked by a gnát.

She máshed it flát

And mándated its ínstant mùmmificátion.

VOCABULARY

máiden	/médIn/	A unmarried woman.
módel	/mádəl/	An example.
gnat	/næt/	A tiny mosquito.
mándate	/mǽndet/	To establish a practice legally. To create a law.
mùmmificátion	/mʌ́mIfIkéšIn/	To preserve a body from rotting.

AN /m/ RIDDLE

Why does that móther cárry her báby?

BECAUSE

The báby refúses to cárry its móther! It's tóo lázy!

A /m/ RHYME

Dávy, Dávy Dúmpling,

Bóil him in the pót.

Súgar him and bútter him

And éat him whíle he's hót.

LEVEL I: AN /m/ & /n/ DIALOGUE: MELANIE & MARCUS

Marcus: Mélanie! I'm húngry!

Melanie: So máke yoursélf a méal.

Marcus: Yóu make it for mé.

Melanie: Dón't be lázy. Máke your ówn lunch.

Marcus: Mé? Make méals? Mel, Í'm gáinfully emplóyed!

Melanie: Lísten, Márc. Yóu may máke the móney, but I run this hóuse.

Marcus: Bút Mél, I'm stárved! Pámper me!

Melanie: Marc, móve yourself intó the kítchen. I'm búsy.

Marcus: Oh, áll right!

Melanie: Thát's my bóy.

VOCABULARY

gáinfully emplóyed	/génfəliyImplɔ́id/	Working for a wage or a salary.
pámper	/pǽmpUr/	To make a fuss over someone, to do everything for them.

LEVEL II/III: AN /m/ DIALOGUE: MELVIN & MARVIN

Marvin: Múst you mángle the magazínes, Mél?

Melvin: Mé? Mángle magazínes?

Marvin: Yés, yóu, you míscreant.

Melvin: Márvin, I recomménd you múll óver your cómment.

Marvin: Máke me!

Melvin: Máster your móods, my fríend. And refráin from júmping the gún.

Marvin: Then whó mútilated my Géntlemen's Mónthly?

Melvin: Mávis's bróod. Emily, Míchael, Melíssa and Míng.

Marvin: Oh, my! The mónsters have stórmed the gátes once móre! Sórry.

Melvin: Everyone mákes mistákes.

VOCABULARY

mángle	/mæηəl/	To tear apart.
míscreant	/mÍskriyInt/	A sinner.
mull óver	/mΛlóvUr/	To think it over.
refráin	/rifrén/	To stop from acting.
júmping the gun	/jΛ́mpiη ðə gΛ́n/	To act in haste, to overreact.
brood	/brud/	A family of siblings (sisters and brothers).
stórmed the gátes	/st⊃rmd ðə géts/	To invade.

THE VOICED BILABIAL GLIDE /w/

Figure 45.

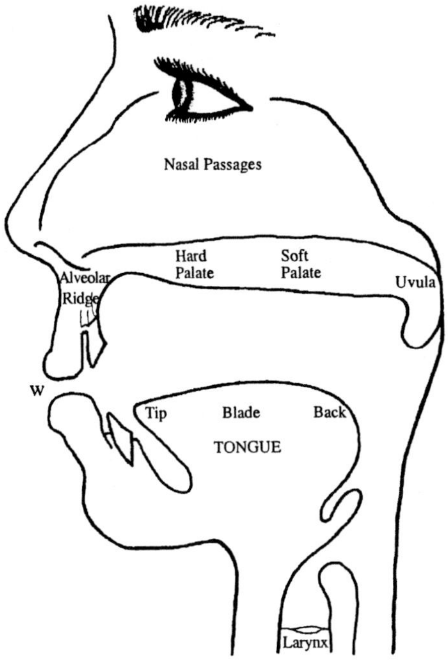

TO ARTICULATE /w/

1. Purse your lips.
2. Leave a tiny opening to let the air out.

REMEMBER: ALPHABET W appears as /w/ in the beginnings and middles of words. It is a vowel sound at the ends of words.

SPEAKING & PHONEME WRITING EXERCISES: /w/

1. To whére are Awílda and Wílma wálking?

2. Whát a wíld-looking wíldflower!

3. Dón't tweak the twins' chéeks.

4. Wórking for wáges is what móst of us dó.

VOCABULARY

tweak /twik/ To lightly pinch someone's cheeks.

A /w/ RIDDLE

Whát tíme of dáy is spelled exáctly the sáme báckward and fórward?

NOON

A /w/ RHYME

Wíllie went wálking one day in the wóods.

Wíllie got lóst. All we fóund were his bóoks.

A /w/ LIMERICK

A wónderful wóman námed Wánda

Was wálking óne day in the <u>túndra</u>.

Shé bumped ínto a <u>crítter</u>

Whó procéeded to hít ’er.

So Wánda whípped it fíner than bútter.

VOCABULARY

<u>crítter</u>	/krÍtUr/	A slang word for creature.
<u>túndra</u>	/tΛ́ndrə/	A cold, mostly treeless plain near the Arctic Circle.

A /w/ TONGUE-TWISTER

Whére in the wórld did Wánda wánder?

Wíll saw her wálking with wállabies Down Under.

VOCABULARY

wállabies	/wáləbiz/	Kangaroos.
Down Under	/daunÁndUr/	Australia.

A /w/ DOGGEREL

Wée Wíllie Wínkie rúns through the tówn.

Upstairs and dównstairs in his níghtgown.

Rápping at the wíndows, shóuting through the lóck.

"Are the chíldren all abéd? It is nów ten o'clóck."

ANOTHER /w/ DOGGEREL

The éensy, wéensy spíder

Climbed úp the wáterspóut.

Dówn came the ráin

And wáshed the spíder óut.

Out came the sún

And dríed up áll the ráin,

And the éensy, wéensy spíder

Climbed úp the spóut agáin.

LEVEL I: A /w/ DIALOGUE: WHITTLING A WOODEN WAGON

Willie: What are you whíttling, Awílda?

Awilda: Oh, hi, Wíllie! I'm whíttling a wágon.

Willie: For yoursélf?

Awilda: The wágon's for Wendy.

Willie: It's so tiny! Will the wheels work?

Awilda: Oh, sure. I'll whíttle the whéels so they túrn.

Willie: Wow! What a wónderful toy!

Awilda: Would you líke to léarn how to whittle?

Willie: Yes!

Awilda: Right nów?

Willie: Yes!

Awilda: Wéll, lét's begín.

VOCABULARY

whíttle	/hwÍtəl/	To carve wood into objects.
wágon	/wǽgIn/	A small or large box on wheels to carry goods and people.

LEVEL II/III: A /w/ TRIALOGUE: WALKING THROUGH THE WOODS IN WINTER

Rowena: Whát a wónderful dáy! I lóve wínter.

Owen: It ís wónderful whén snów blánkets the wílderness.

William: If you réally wánt to knów, I'd ráther be sómeplace wárm.

Owen: Why, Wílliam! You lóve wínter spórts!

William: I do. But the wéather nówadays is tóo glácial.

Rowena: Oh, Wílliam! Yóu're álways compláining abóut the wéather!

William: Wéll, we áll have our wéaknesses. Míne's whíning.

Rowena: And you dó it véry wéll, tóo.

Owen: The wéather's túrning. Lét's decíde whéther to cámp óut óvernight.

William: Oh, nó you dón't! Wé're góing back to the cábin ríght nów!

Owen: Júst kídding, Will. Cóme on, fólks. Báck to the cábin.

VOCABULARY

blánkets	/blǽŋkIts/	Covers completely.
wílderness	/wÍldUrnIs/	The forests where only animals live.
glácial	/gléšəl/	Extremely cold.
whíning	/hwáiniŋ/	Complaining nasally, as though you have a cold.

THE TWO LABIO-DENTAL FRICATIVES: /f/ & /v/

VOICELESS /f/ & VOICED /v/

TO ARTICULATE /f/ & /v/

1. Lift the upper lip so that the upper teeth are visible.
2. Pull in the lower lip so that the upper teeth can bite it.
3. Squeeze the air out of your mouth.
4. Curl your tongue up towards the alveolar ridge.

Figure 46.

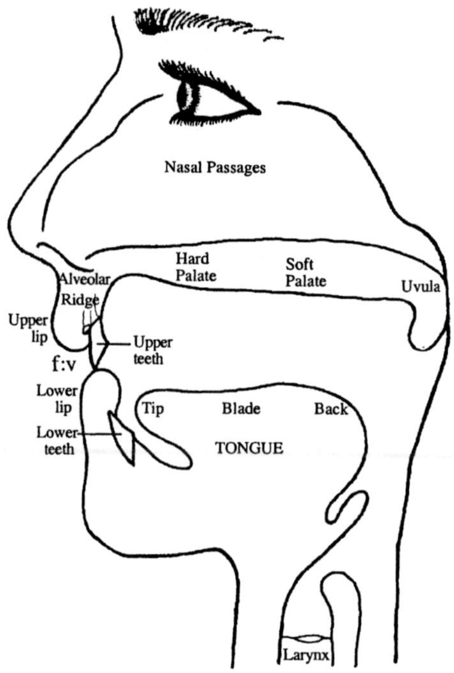

SPEAKING & PHONEME WRITING EXERCISES: /f/

1. Phíl's <u>fámous</u> for his fúnny jókes.

2. Effie's <u>síft</u>ing the flour fínely.

3. Wátch the <u>púff pástry</u> líft.

4. Fránces Fármer flíes <u>fíghter plánes</u>.

VOCABULARY

<u>fámous</u>	/fémIs/	To be very well known. Everyone knows who you are.
<u>sift</u>	/sIft/	To push flour through a sieve (a mesh), for baking cakes.
<u>púff pástry</u>	/pΛ́f péstri/	A very light, very thin dough for cream puffs.
<u>fíghter plánes</u>	/fáitUr pláns/	War planes.

AN /f/ RIDDLE

What has fóur wheels and flíes?

A GARBAGE TRUCK

ANOTHER /f/ RIDDLE

Why can't a fóx fly like a fálcon?

THE VIXEN WON'T LET HIM!

VOCABULARY

fox	/fax/	A dog-like animal with reddish fur and a pointed face.
fálcon	/fǽlkIn/:/fɔ́lkIn/	A small, eagle-like bird used to hunt other birds.
víxen	/vÍksIn/	A female fox. The male is called a dog fox.

AN /f/ RHYME

Fíddle-dee-dée, fíddle-dee-dée

The fly has flústered the búmble bée.

The bée forgáve the fóolish fly

Then fléw off to fínd fresh flówers for téa.

ANOTHER /f/ RHYME

A fléa and a fly in a flúe,

Wére imprísoned, so whát did they dó?

Sáid the fléa, "Lét us fly."

Sáid the fly, "Lét us flée."

So they fléw through the flóor of the flúe.

VOCABULARY

flea	/fli/	A tiny, high-jumping insect that lives on the blood of animals.
flue	/flu/	The pipe leading from a stove, carrying smoke outdoors.
imprísoned	/?ImprÍzInd/	To be jailed. To be in prison /?In prÍzIn/ means to be in jail.
flee	/fli/	To run away very fast.

SPEAKING & PHONEME WRITING EXERCISES: /v/

1. Véry well, Véra. We'll vísit Válerie todáy.

2. Everyóne of us would lóve to líve well.

3. Vóila! I've wón! I'm victórious!

4. Víncent vóws he'll trím the grápevines.

VOCABULARY

voilá	/vwalá/	A French word meaning Hooray!
víctor	/vÍktUr/	The person who has won a contest.
vow	/vau/	A promise that cannot be broken.

A /v/ LIMERICK

There wás a vámpire from Vladivóstak,

Véry táll, óveractive, and a hemophíliac.

His véstments were quite ícky,

Fílthy, táttered and stícky

And his fángs were encrústed with pláque.

VOCABULARY

Vladivóstak	/vlàdIvɔ́stak/	A city in Russia.
hemophíliac	/himofíliyæk/	A person who bleeds and cannot stop.
véstments	/vɛ́stmInts/	Clothes priests wear in holy places.
tátters	/tǽtUrz/	Clothes that are torn into shreds or bits.
fílthy	/fÍlθi/	Very, very dirty.
fángs	/fæŋz/	Long upper teeth.
stícky	/stÍki/	Gummy.
encrústed	/?Inkrʌ́stId/	To be coated or covered with a hard shell.
pláque	/plæk/	The white coating on your teeth the dentist scrapes off.

TWO /v/ RIDDLES

1. Whát is vérsatile, váriable and néver léaves?

THE WEATHER

2. Whát did the víal say to the vámpire?

YOU ARE VILE!

VOCABULARY

vérsatile	/vÚrsətayəl/	To be able to do a lot of activities very well.
váriable	/vériyəbəl/	To be changeable.
víal	/váyəl/	A small bottle for perfume or pills.
víle	/váyəl/	To be worse than disgusting.
vámpire	/vǽmpayUr/	A creature that sucks blood.

A /v/ RHYME

Every végetable on which Vílma smíles

Vínes and twínes through her cómpost piles.

Vibúrnum, vióla, verbéna and vétch

Fínd rich róotings in that víle-smélling créche.

VOCABULARY

cómpost	/kámpost/	Rotting vegetables, manure, ashes: garden food.
vibúrnum	/vaibÚrnəm/	An evergreen shrub with sweet-smelling flowers.
vióla	/vayólə/	A small, purple face-like flower.
verbéna	/vUrbínə/	A multi-colored tiny-flowered plant.
vetch	/vɛč/	A low-growing plant that puts nitrogen in the soil.
créche	/krɛš/	A baby's cradle without rockers. A baby basket.

LEVEL I/II: AN /f/ TRIALOGUE: FLORENCE, PHILIP & FRANZ

Franz:	Héy, fríends. Háve you séen Ophélia?
Philip:	Ophélia whó?
Florence:	Ophélia Fóster, that fúnny magícian . . .
Franz:	The óne who fáked out Fránk Fontáine last Fríday.
Florence:	She cálls hersélf Phílly Fóster, the Fábulous Fémale Fakír.
Philip:	Whát does she dó?
Franz:	Wéll, she preténds to fúmble.
Florence:	She delíberately góofs up her áct.
Franz:	And júst when you fáncy she's góing to fáil. . . .
Florence:	She cómes through like a tróoper.
Philip:	What a gal!

VOCABULARY

fake out	/fékaut/	To fool someone.
fakír	/fékír/	A Hindu word for "magician."
fúmble	/fʌ́mbəl/	To drop an object by mistake.
goof	/guf/	To make a mistake.
fáncy	/fǽnsi/	To think.
tróoper	/trúpUr/	A foot soldier. Someone who gets things done with dignity.

LEVEL I/II: A /v/ DIALOGUE: YOUNG LOVE

Vernice: Évan, ísn't it gréat to be in lóve?

Evan: It súre is! Évelyn and I have béen in lóve foréver.

Vernice: Háven't you just mét?

Evan: We mét last Fríday. But it féels like forév̀er.

Vernice: Óliver and I have been in lóve for fíve years.

Evan: I knów. Wów, Verníce! It begán when you were bóth séven.

Vernice: Yóung love.

Evan: Véry young love.

Vernice: I hope you and Évelyn will be very happy.

Evan: Thanks. We hope so, too.

NOTE: Evan and Evelyn can be pronounced two different ways. /?ɛ́vɪn/ or /?ívɪn/ and /?ɛ́vəlɪn/ or /?ívəlɪn/.

THE FOUR PALATO-VELAR
CONSONANTS: /k & /g/ & /ŋ/ & /y/

Figure 47.

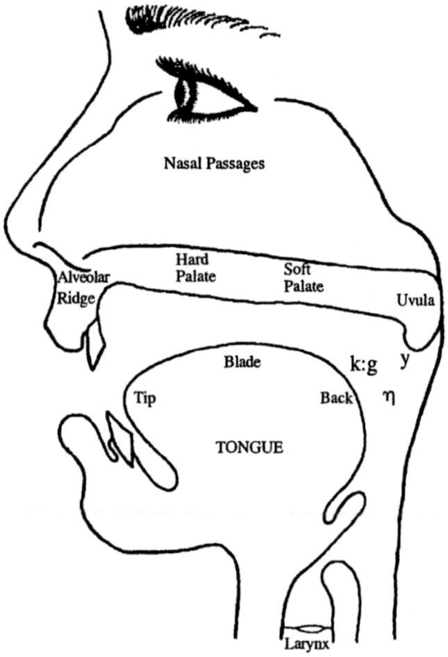

Figure 48.

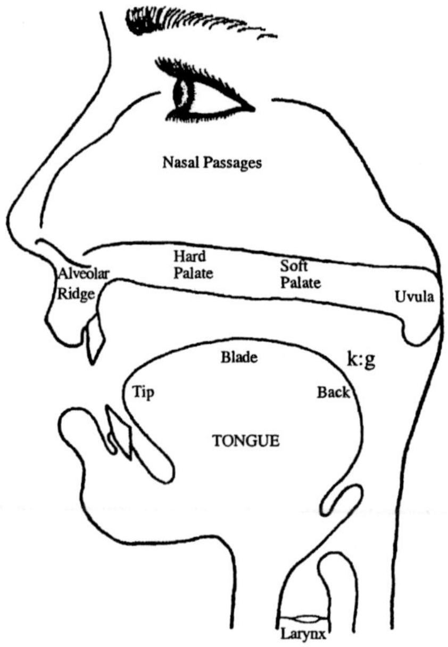

THE TWO PALATO-VELAR STOPS /k/ & /g/

VOICELESS /k/ and VOICED /g/ are PLOSIVE STOPS.

TO ARTICULATE /k/ & /g/

1. Squeeze the back-of-the-mouth/velar muscles.
2. Raise the back of the tongue and bounce it against the soft palate.
3. Allow the air to explode.

SPEAKING & PHONEME WRITING CONTRAST EXERCISES: /k/ & /g/

VOICED /g/	VOICELESS /k/
1a. Keep góing, Glénda.	1b. Kélly's cóoking <u>cóq au vín</u>.
2a. Agáin? Góodness grácious!	2b. Kéep the kítten wárm.
3a. Give Glória her glóves.	3b. Míchael cleans cónstantly.
4a. Gílda Rádner's a gréat comédian.	4b. Cróss-country skíing is cóol.

VOCABULARY

<u>cóq au vín</u> /kɔ́kɔvǽn/ A French recipe for cooking chicken in red wine.

A /k/ & /g/ LIMERICK

A cúte little gírl from Killárney,

Was quíte gífted in díshing out blárney.

Whíle pássing 'róund her púrse,

She'd convérse in frée vérse,

Collécting more gélt than she could cárry.

VOCABULARY

Killárney	/kIlárni/	A district in Ireland.
díshing out	/dÍšiŋaut/	Giving.
blárney	/blárni/	An Irish Gaelic word for very well spoken.
purse	/pUrs/	A small pocketbook.
convérse	/kənvUrs/	To speak with someone.
frée vérse	/frívUrs/	A form of poetry that doesn't rhyme.
gelt	/gɛlt/	Money.

A /k/ & /g/ RIDDLE

Púrple, yéllow, réd and gréen.

The kíng cánnot réach it, nor yét the quéen.

Nór cán Óld Nóll whose pówer is gréat.

Answer this ríddle while I cóunt to éight.

A RAINBOW.

VOCABULARY

Óld Nóll	/ʔóld nál/	A name for the devil.

A /k/ DOGGEREL

Róck-a-bye báby   ón the tréetop.

Whén the wínd blóws   the crádle will róck.

Whén the bóugh bréaks   the crádle will fáll,

And dówn will come báby,   bóugh, crádle and áll.

VOCABULARY

crádle	/krédəl/	A small, wooden rocking bed for a baby.
bough	/bo/ or /bau/	A thick tree branch.

A /k/ LIMERICK

Quéen Clotílde was quíte a comédian.

She quípped cléver gíbes at the Philistínians

Who thóught art was crúd-o

And ópera vócal gúmbo,

And dánce of ány kind óbscene-ian.

VOCABULARY

quípped	/kwÍpt/	Made a joke.
gibes	/ǰaibz/	Poking fun at someone.
Philistinians	/fIlIstÍniyInz/	People who dislike Western high culture. It is also the name of an ancient seafaring people who lived in Israel.
crud	/krʌd/	Sticky, gummy stuff.
gúmbo	/gʌ́mbo/	A New Orleans okra-based stew.
obscéne	/ʔabsín/	Disgusting.

AN 1870S ENGLISH MUSIC HALL SONG

MY GRANDFATHER'S CLOCK

My grándfather's clóck was too bíg for the shélf,

So it stóod nínety yéars on the flóor.

It was táller by hálf than the óld mán himsélf,

But it wéighed nót a pénnyweight móre.

It was bóught on the mórn of the dáy that he was bórn

And it néver let óff télling tíme.

But it stópped. Shórt. Néver to gó agáin

Whén the óld mán díed.

Nínety yéars withóut stúmbling.

Tíck tóck tíck tóck.

His lífe's séconds númbering.

Tíck tóck tíck tóck.

It stópped. Shórt. Néver to gó agáin

Whén the óld mán díed.

NOTE: The British music hall was like American vaudville. All kinds of acts were performed, such as magic, comedy, dancing and singing.

VOCABULARY

grándfather's clock	/grǽndfáðUrz klák/	A clock that stands on the floor.
pénnyweight	/péniwet/	A way to measure nails.

LEVEL I: A /k/ & /g/ DIALOGUE: INCONSIDERATE GUESTS

Gloria: Kéith, where áre you?

Keith: In the garáge. Why?

Gloria: Our cómpany is cóming up the róad!

Keith: They're twó hóurs éarly!

Gloria: Of áll the ínconsiderate people! Come ón. Lét's get góing.

Keith: But I'm cóvered in gúnk!

Gloria: And I'm cóoking up a stórm! I knów! We'll hide!

Keith: Tóo láte. Théy're át the gáte. Whát'll we dó now?

Gloria: Gíve it úp. We'll háve to máke the bést of it.

Keith: I knów! Lét's pút them to wórk.

Gloria: Our guésts?

Keith: You gót it!

Glenda: Gréat idéa!

3 PHONEME NOTES ON ALPHABET LETTER g

ALPHABET LETTER g has at least 3 different sounds.

1. /g/ 2. /ǰ/ 3. /ž/

1. /g/ & 2. /ǰ/ occur in the beginnings, middles, and ends of words.

3. /ž/ which comes from French, appears mostly at the ends of words. See Apico-Alveolar Fricatives /š/ & /ž/, pages 110–114.

1. /g/	2. /ǰ/
grow agáin díalogue	gérbil búdget ledge

3. /ž/

garáge barráge colláge

PHONEME NOTES ON ALPHABET LETTER x

ALPHABET LETTER x can be pronounced in 2 ways.

1. VOICELESS /ks/ or 2. VOICED /gz/.

NOTE: 1. /ks/ appears most of the time when ALPHABET LETTER x is preceded by ALPHABET LETTER e and is followed by ALPHABET LETTER c or by another consonant, such as t.
2. /gz/ appears mostly between 2 vowels or a vowel & h.

ALPHABET LETTER X

1. /ks/		2. /gz/	
éxcellent	excépt	exáctly	examinátion
excéed	extént	exámple	exért
extínct	excéll	exhíbit	exággerate

LEVEL I/II: A /ks/ & /gz/ DIALOGUE: I'M EXHAUSTED!

Axel:	Bíggs, I'm exháusted!
Biggs:	What exháusted you, Axel?
Axel:	I júst had an áwful éxaminátion.
Biggs:	An exám? In whát?
Axel:	In chémistry. The exám was áll expériments.
Biggs:	Wéll, Áxel, you háven't died yét.
Axel:	I expéct to, thóugh, in exáctly síx mínutes.
Biggs:	I'm súre you did éxcellently.
Axel:	My lífe is over!
Biggs:	Nót just yét. Come ón. Lét's gó for a rún in the párk.
Axel:	A run! Is thát all you can sáy?
Biggs:	A rún will do you good. Lét's go.

VOCABULARY

exháusted	/ʔɛgzɔ́stId/	Very, very tired.
chémistry	/kɛ́mIstri/	A science where chemicals are mixed to create new ones.
expériments	/ʔɛkspɛ́rImInts/	Tests to prove or disprove an idea.

THE VOICED VELAR NASAL /η/

Figure 49.

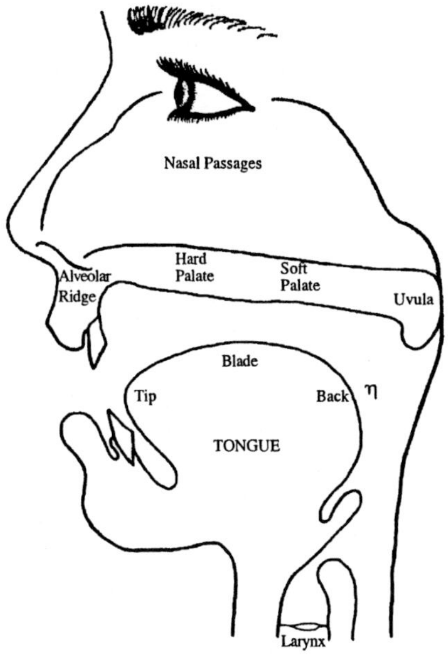

TO ARTICULATE /η/

1. Press the back of the tongue against the velum/uvula & close the air passage.

SPEAKING & PHONEME WRITING EXERCISES: /η/

1. Díng dóng. Ríng the béll.
2. Síng me a sóng, oh, bírd of spríng.
3. Mr. Díngle dréw a tríangle in pínk ink.
4. My ánkle tíngles.

PHONEME:SPELLING NOTE: n + k = ηk

When /η/ is followed by a /k/, as in "ínk," PHONEME /k/ follows /η/.

rink sank blink trínket stink wink think

AN /η/ RIDDLE

As I lóoked at my wíndow, I lóoked through my gólden ring.

I sáw the déad cárrying the líving. Wásn't that a wóndrous thing?

A TRAINFUL OF PEOPLE

AN /ɳ/ RHYME

Síng, síng. Whát shall I síng?

The cát's run awáy with the púdding string.

Dó, dó. Whát shall I dó?

The cát's run awáy with the púdding, tóo!

VOCABULARY

púdding	/pÚdiɳ/	A food made of fat, meat, raisins, spices and tied in a ball.
string	/striɳ/	A thin piece of rope.

AN /ɳ/ LIMERICK

A fínk of kíng named Díngle-a-ling,

Would téase young ládies ínto thínk-a-ling,

That he'd wéd them in a wínk.

Till óne day óne lass blínked,

And lassóoed him ínto gíving her a ríng-a-ling.

VOCABULARY

fink	/fíɳk/	A nasty liar.
tease	/tíz/	To fool or make fun of someone.
wed	/wɛd/	To marry.
lass	/læs/	A young woman, a teenager.
blink	/bliɳk/	To flutter one's eyelashes.
lassóo	/læsú/	To capture a person or an animal by throwing a rope around it.

AN /ŋ/ DOGGEREL

Díng, dóng, ríng the béll.

Pússy's swímming in the wéll.

I thínk that bád boy Jímmy Hínks

Threw pússy down that déep, déep sínk.

AN /ŋ/ RHYME

Hárry lost his wédding ring

Wáshing his hánds at the kítchen sink.

Lúcy then léft to go júnketing,

To Hóng Kóng, Macáo, and of course, Nankíng.

AN /ŋ/ DOGGEREL

Déedle, déedle dúmpling, my son Jóhn,

Wént to béd with his stóckings ón.

One shoe óff, óne shoe ón,

Déedle, déedle dúmpling, my son Jóhn.

LEVEL I/II: A /ŋ/ DIALOGUE: BINKY & STINKY

Binky:	It's spríng! The bírds are <u>on the wíng</u>! Lísten to them síng!
Stinky:	Bínky! Gó back to sléep. It's twó a.m. in the mórning!
Binky:	Dóesn't it máke you <u>tíngle</u>?
Stinky:	Tíngle! The stárs are stíll <u>twínkling</u>! I wánt my fórty wínks.
Binky:	I'm góing to <u>ánkle</u> thróugh the <u>déw</u>, <u>míngle</u> with náture.
Stinky:	Gó míngle. Lét me sléep.
Binky:	Lét's nót <u>brángle</u>. Súre you won't jóin me?
Stinky:	Yóu slínk through the <u>júngle</u>. I'll sínk intó <u>Mórpheus</u>'s árms.
Binky:	Spóil sport!

VOCABULARY

<u>on the wing</u>	/ʔanðəwíŋ/	Flying.
<u>tíngle</u>	/tíngəl/	When your skin vibrates, or your nerves jump.
<u>twínkling</u>	/twíŋkliŋ/	Flashing on and off.
<u>ankle</u>	/ʔǽŋkəl/	To walk.
<u>déw</u>	/du/	The early morning moisture (water) that covers plants.
<u>míngle</u>	/míŋəl/	To mix with.
<u>brángle</u>	/brǽŋəl/	A fussy kind of argument.
<u>slink</u>	/sliŋk/	To slide like a snake.
<u>júngle</u>	/ǰʌ́ŋəl/	A tropical forest.
<u>Mórpheus</u>	/mɔ́rfiyəs/	The Greek god of sleep.

LEVEL I/II: A /ŋ/ DIALOGUE: RING AROUND RINGO

Ringo:	Anke, háve you séen my díamond ring?
Anke:	The ríng Dánko gave you?
Ringo:	Thát's the óne. Háve you séen it?
Anke:	Dídn't you bríng it to the jéweler to pólish?
Ringo:	I distínctly remémber pícking it up yésterday mórning.
Anke:	I thínk you sáid you were góing to wear it to Angie's wédding.
Ringo:	Thát's tomórrow évening. Hélp me fínd the ríng.
Anke:	Ríngo! Lóok! It's ón your fínger!
Ringo:	I've been wéaring it all alóng?
Anke:	Whát a díng-a-ling.
Ringo:	Wéll! I guéss I shóuld be thánking you.
Anke:	I guéss you shóuld.
Ringo:	Okáy. Thánks.
Anke:	Yóu're wélcome.

Figure 50.

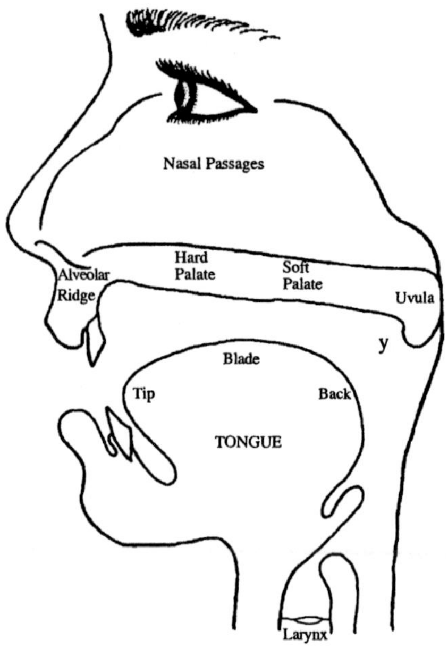

TO ARTICULATE /y/

1. Pull the back of the tongue up against the lower edge of the soft palate.
2. Press the sides of the tongue the insides of the upper molars.

SPEAKING & PHONEME WRITING EXERCISES: /y/

1. I'm flying to Yálta diréctly.

2. Wé creáte beaútiful músic, yóu and I.

3. Okay, yóungsters. Pláy the trío in únison.

4. In my opínion utópian socíeties are únrealístic.

VOCABULARY

Yálta	/yɔ́ltə/	A city in the Crimea in southern Russia, on the Black Sea.
únison	/yúnisIn/	Together.
utópian	/yutópiyIn/	Perfection.

A /y/ RHYME

Beaútiful músic is álways so glórious!

Amúsing, allúring, the sóunds so luxúrious!

VOCABULARY

glórious	/glɔ́riyəs/	Absolutely wonderful.
allúring	/ʔəlyúriŋ/ or /ʔəlúriŋ/	Very, very attractive.
luxúrious	/lʌ́gžúriyIs/	Richly comfortable.

A /y/ LIMERICK

A yénta who dréssed áll in yéllow,

Was knówn to hóller and béllow

At áll of the spóngers,

Who wánted to expúnge her

Of her míllions, those évil yóung féllows

VOCABULARY

yénta	/yɛ́nta/	A Yiddish word meaning a person who gossips a lot.
béllow	/bɛ́lo/	To yell, but in a deep voice.
spónger	/spΛnǰUr/	Someone who lives off others & does not work at all.
expúnge	/ʔɛkspΛ́nǰ/	To take away, steal, remove.

A /y/ RHYME

Hígher and hígher the kite ascénded,

In the quíet of the sétting sun.

The flying kite, as dáy was done,

Swóoped dówn to earth, bélly-up, up-énded.

VOCABULARY

ascénded	/ʔəsɛ́ndId/	Rose up. Climbed up.
swoop	/swup/	To fly in a curve or a semi-circle.

3 PHONEME:SPELLING NOTES ON ALPHABET LETTER y

1. ALPHABET LETTER y as a CONSONANT

2. ALPHABET LETTER y as a VOWEL

3. INVISIBLE /y/

1. When ALPHABET LETTER y appears at the beginnings and ends of words and is followed by a vowel, it is pronounced /y/.

/y___/			/___y___/	
yell	yéllow	yúmmy	convéyance	káyo
yes	young	you	portráying	obéying

2. When ALPHABET LETTER y appears at the ends of words, it is pronounced as a vowel sound in both singular & plural.
   a. /i/
   b. /e/
   c. /I/ or
   d. DIPHTHONG /ai/

	a. /___i/		b. /___e/		d. /___ai/	
SINGULAR:	bérry	fúnny	reláy	pláy	fly	try
PLURAL:	bérries	fúnnies	reláys	plays	flies	tries

c. When ALPHABET LETTER y appears in a word that comes from GREEK, the VOWEL PHONEMES are /I/ or

d. /ai/.

c. /I/		d. /ai/	
synchrónic	sympathétic	hypochóndriac	psychólogy
hypnotism	mystery	gynecólogy	hybrid

NOTE: See Chapter II, pages 77–79 for NOT-A-DIPHTHONG INVISIBLE y.

3. INVISIBLE /y/ occurs in many words that pronounce /y/ even though ALPHABET LETTER y is not written in.

The 2 most common clues are

a. ALPHABET LETTER u at the beginnings and in the middles of words, and

b. combinations of ALPHABET VOWELS, such as ia, ie, io.

a. /yu___/

utópian úsually úseful útility

usúrp únion uníque úniform

NOTE: Many words of French origin with an ALPHABET CONSONANT followed by ALPHABET LETTER u, have an INVISIBLE /y/ between the ALPHABET CONSONANT and ALPHABET VOWEL u: /C+yu/.

/C+yu/

cúte músic pew cúre dúty néws

búreau fúry cúrious infúsion neúron pure

VOCABULARY

pew	/pyu/	A bench most often found in a church.

b. INVISIBLE /y/ very often appears in words with the following combinations of ALPHABET VOWELS:

1. __ious 2. __ior 3. __ea__ 4. __ie__

5. __ia__ 6. __io__ 7. __eau 8. __(a)eo

The most common pronunciation pattern is to sound out PHONEME /y/ between two of the ALPHABET VOWELS, creating another syllable.

1. __ious

/iyəs/

cúrious sérious

2. __ior

/iyUr/

inférior extérior

3. __ea__

/iye/ /iyə/

creáte Koréa idéa

4. __ie__

/áyIt/ /yu/

díet quíet revíew renew

5. __ia__

/áyə/ /ayæ/

vía díal tríad Siám

6. __io__

/ayə/

violín líon

7. __ea

/__iyæ/

beátify

8. __(a)eo

/__iya/

archaeólogy géology

NOTE: INVISIBLE y is also common in what seem to be single-syllable words ending in SYLLABIC /əl/ and SYLLABIC /Ur/. See Chapter II, page 77 & Chapter III, pages 123, 132–134.

/áyəl/

vile stýle

/awər/

flóur sóur

/ɔyəl/

bóil dóily

LEVEL I/II: A /y/ DIALOGUE: YES, YES, YES!

Yolanda: Dídn't I téll you your plán wouldn't wórk?

Yetta: Yés, you díd.

Yolanda: Yet you stíll haven't retúrned the yárn.

Yetta: Dón't yéll, Yolánda!

Yolanda: That yéllowish cólor looks yúcky on yóu.

Yetta: Dón't rub it ín.

Yolanda: And it is sériously óverpriced, tóo.

Yetta: But the wóol is só luxúrious! Réal cashmére!

Yolanda: Yétta, dón't you réalize you were préssured into búying it?

Yetta: I guéss so.

Yolanda: Wéll? Why are you deláying?

Yetta: Yóu are a búlly Yolánda.

Yolanda: I'm búllying you for your ówn sake. Réady?

Yetta: Yés. Yés. Yés. Yés. Yés!

LEVEL II/III: A /y/ DIALOGUE: SIGHTSEEING IN NEW YORK

Beatrice: Míles, lét's vísit a muséum todáy.

Miles: I'd ráther hear some músic, Béa.

Beatrice: Músic toníght and a muséum todáy. Okáy?

Miles: Fine. Whích muséum do you wánt to vísit?

Beatrice: The Fíre Muséum. And a fíre house.

Miles: Whý are you só inspíred by fíre?

Beatrice: I'm jóining the voluntéer fíre brigáde at hóme.

Miles: You súre seem enthusiástic abóut fíre.

Beatrice: Cóme ón!

Miles: Okáy, but toníght we eat dínner in a piáno bar. Déal?

Beatrice: It's a déal.

VOCABULARY

muséum	/myuzíyəm/	A building that houses objects of art, past & present.
fíre house	/fáyUr háus/	A building housing fire-fighters and their trucks.
inspíred	/?InspáyUrd/	Encouraged to act on an idea.
voluntéer	/v*a*ləntír/	Someone who offers to work without pay.
brigáde	/brIgéd/	A military group.
piáno bar	/piyǽnob*a*r/	A restaurant where someone plays the piano.

THE GLOTTALS /ʔ/ & /h/

/ʔ/ is a VOICED STOP and /h/ is VOICELESS FRICATIVE.

Figure 51.

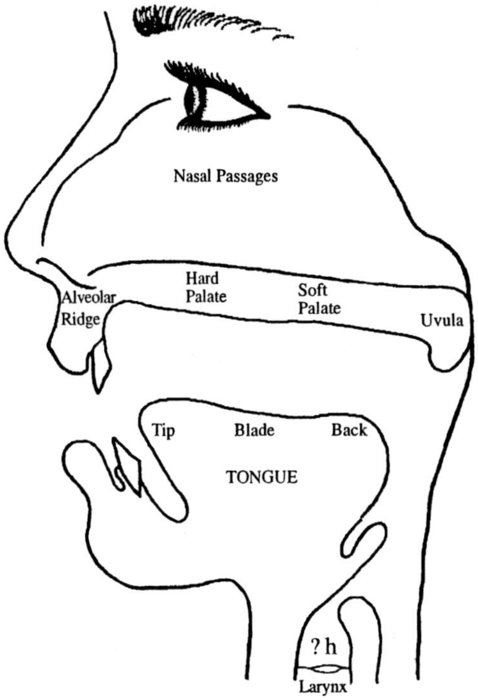

TO ARTICULATE /ʔ/

1. Stop the air, then release it by contracting the vocal cords.

TO ARTICULATE /h/

1. Squeeze the air.

SPEAKING & PHONEME WRITING EXERCISES: /ʔ/

1. I cán't get my áct together.

2. Báalbek is an áncient árcheological site.

3. Every óne of us has at léast óne próblem.

4. An ápple a dáy kéeps the dóctor awáy.

VOCABULARY

Báalbek	/báʔalbɛk/	A city in Lebanon that existed about 2,500 years ago.
áncient	/ʔénšInt/	Very, very, very old.
árcheological	/ʔarkiyəlájIkəl/	From Greek, meaning old learning.
site	/sait/	A location.

NOTE: Both /ʔ/ & /h/ occur at the beginnings and in the middles of words.

A GLOTTAL STOP /ʔ/ PRONUNCIATION PATTERN

Except at the BEGINNINGS of words, English drops the GLOTTAL STOP /ʔ/. When a word ends in a CONSONANT PHONEME and the word that follows begins with an ALPHABET VOWEL (a,e,i,o,u), then

1. the GLOTTAL STOP /ʔ/ is dropped and
2. the CONSONANT PHONEME takes over, making two words sound like one.

NOTE: See INVISIBLE /y/ pages 176–178.

---

1. I cán't get my act together.

WITH /ʔ/

ʔai kǽnt gɛt mai ʔǽkt tugɛ́ðUr

WITHOUT /ʔ/

ʔai kǽnt gɛt mayǽkt tugɛ́ðUr

2. Baalbeck is an ancient archaeological site.

WITH /ʔ/

báʔalbɛk ʔIz ʔæn ʔénšInt ʔárkiyəláǰIkəl sáit

WITHOUT /ʔ/

bálbɛkIzænénšIntářkiyəláǰIkəl sáit

3. Every óne of us has at léast óne próblem.

WITH /ʔ/

ʔɛ́vri wʌ́n ʔəv ʔʌs hǽz ʔæt líst wʌ́n prábləm

WITHOUT /ʔ/

ʔɛ́vri wʌ́n əvʌs hǽzæt líst wʌ́n prábləm

4. An ápple a dáy kéeps the dóctor awáy.

WITH /ʔ/

ʔæn ʔǽpəl ʔə dé kíps ðə dáktUr ʔəwé

WITHOUT /ʔ/

ʔænǽpələ dé kíps ðə dáktUrəwé

FIND /ʔ/ IN THIS LIMERICK

An éxtra-large égg sáw an ápple,

Whíle atténding a wédding in a <u>chápel</u>.

She fell ínstantly in lóve-a

With this bríght <u>Casanóva</u>.

But her lóve came to <u>náught</u>.

The ápple was <u>snápped up</u> by Snápple.

VOCABULARY

<u>chápel</u>	/čæpǽl/	A small church.
<u>Casanóva</u>	/kæsənóvə/	A storybook man who made love to lots of women.
<u>naught</u>	/n⊃t/	Nothing.
<u>snápped up</u>	/snǽptΛp/	Grabbed quickly.

FIND /ʔ/ IN THIS RHYME

Oh, the gránd old Dúke of Yórk,

He hád ten thóusand mén,

He márched them úp to the tóp of the híll,

And he márched them dówn agáin.

And whén they were úp, they were úp,

And whén they were dówn, they were dówn,

And whén they ónly hálf-way úp

They were néither úp nor dówn.

FIND /ʔ/ IN THIS DOGGEREL

I bóught a dózen néw-laid éggs

From góod old Farmer Díckens.

I dállied home ’pon my two légs

And fóund them fúll of chíckens.

VOCABULARY

dállied	/dǽlid/	Took one’s time.
’pon	/pon/	A contraction for upon.

A MIDDLE ENGLISH FOLKSONG: GREENSLEEVES

Alás, my lóve, you dó me wróng,

To cást me óut discóurteously.

Fór I have lóved you só lóng,

Delíghting in your cómpany.

CHORUS:

Gréensleeves was áll my jóy,

Gréensleeves was my delíght.

Gréensleeves was my hárt of góld,

Whó but my lády Gréensleeves.

VOCABULARY

gréensleeves	/grínslivz/	Only the wealthy could afford colorful clothing.
discóurteously	/diskÚrtiyəsli/	To be rude, unmannerly.
hart	/hart/	A young deer, about two years old.

LEVEL I/II: AN /?/ DIALOGUE: EGGS AT EVERY MEAL!

Agnes: I adóre eggs!

Oliver: But eggs at évery méal?

Agnes: They're só áppetizing!

Oliver: Ágnes, you're óff your rócker!

Agnes: Eggs are éxcellent édibles. Fúll of nútrients.

Oliver: Enóugh is enóugh! They're tóo much of a góod thing.

Agnes: Óliver, you are só ígnorant!

Oliver: Bóy, your cholésterol lévels must be hígh!

Agnes: Actually, they're júst where they shóuld be.

Oliver: Néver árgue with an égg áddict.

VOCABULARY

adóre	/?ədɔ́r/	To love someone or something very, very much.
édibles	/?ɛ́dIbəlz/	Anything that can be eaten.
áppetizing	/?ǽpItaiziŋ/	Very tasty.
óff your rócker	/?ɔ́f y⊃rákUr/	A little crazy.
nútrients	/nútriyInts/	Full of vitamins.
ígnorant	/?ÍgnUrInt/	Doesn't know anything.
cholésterol	/kəlɛ́stUrol/	Different kinds of fats in the bloodstream.
áddict	/?ǽdIkt/	Dependent upon a thing, like cigarettes.

LEVEL I/II: AN /ʔ/ DIALOGUE: AN EXCITING EVENT

Irma:	Állison, I'm invíted to an excíting evént.
Allison:	How <u>intríguing</u>, Írma! Whát's it all abóut?
Irma:	An <u>assóciate</u> at my láw firm is táking matérnity leave.
Allison:	Whén's her báby arríving?
Irma:	He's adópting an éight-year-old bóy.
Allison:	By himsélf?
Irma:	Áll by himsélf.
Allison:	Whát a góod idéa!
Irma:	I agrée. Hé'll be an éxcellent párent.
Allison:	Whát are you gíving him?
Irma:	Cash. Anyone who has chíldren álways needs éxtra móney.
Allison:	I agrée. Unléss you're <u>afflúent</u>, móney is the bést gift.

VOCABULARY

<u>afflúent</u>	/ʔə flúwInt/	Wealthy.
<u>intríguing</u>	/ʔIntrígiη/	Very, very interesting.
<u>assóciate</u>	/ʔə sóšIt/	A lawyer who is not a partner in the firm.

Figure 52.

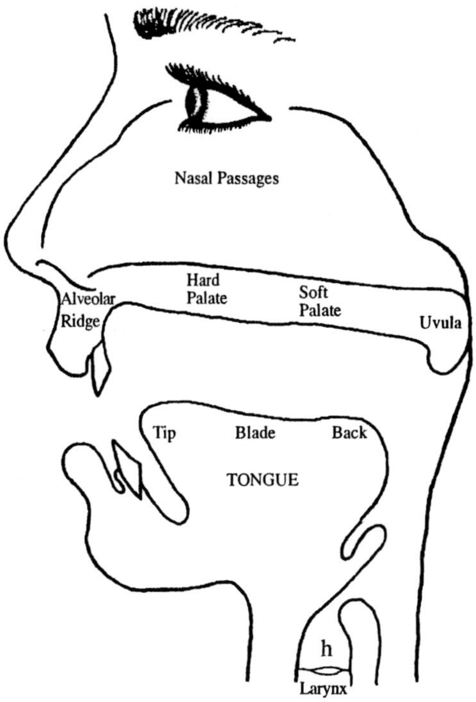

TO ARTICULATE /h/

1. Squeeze the air (whisper).

SPEAKING & PHONEME WRITING EXERCISES: /h/

1. I héar Hélen is háving twins.

2. Háve you héard abóut Hárry's hóliday in Havána?

3. He háppens to háve twó houses.

4. Hénry's véry háppy. His héart is fine.

A /h/ RHYME

Hárry's <u>mate</u> was ín great néed.

He néeded Hárry to hélp him <u>héave</u>

A héavy dóllhouse his síster belíeved

Belónged to hér and nót to her níece.

VOCABULARY

<u>mate</u> /met/ A friend or marriage partner/spouse.
<u>heave</u> /hiv/ To lift and throw a heavy object.

FIND /h/ IN THIS RIDDLE

Hów did the hén háppen to líve in a háunted hénhouse?

SHE INHERITED IT FROM HER HUSBAND

FIND /?/ & /h/ IN THIS WHOSE/WHO'S RHYME

Whóse is that adórable, angélic hórse?

It's ówned by Hélen Evángeline.

Who's ríding that amázing hórse?

I am. Amánda Elízabeth Apperdine.

FIND /?/ & /h/ RHYME

Yóu find mílk and I'll find flóur,

And wé'll have a púdding in hálf-an-hóur.

FIND /?/ & /h/ IN THIS RHYME

The gíant Jim, he's a gíant, grim.

He wéars a hát withóut a brím.

He wéighs a tón, and wéars a blóuse,

But he trémbles when he sées a móuse!

LEVEL I/II: AN /ʔ/ & /h/ DIALOGUE: HANGING OUT AT THE HOSPITAL

Henry: Húrry úp, Héttie.

Hettie: Húrry up for whát, Hénry?

Henry: We're hánging óut at the hóspital.

Hettie: Hánging out whére?

Henry: At Hóllyhock Háven.

Hettie: That húge house on Hóllyhock Hill?

Henry: Hánnah's pláying her hárp for the pátients.

Hettie: And wé'll just háng aróund?

Henry: We'll síng alóng and gíve the hélp a hánd.

Hettie: Whát a nice idéa. Húrry up, Hénry.

Henry: Huh!

VOCABULARY

hánging out	/hæŋiŋáut/	Meeting friends and socializing.
harp	/hɑrp/	A very large stringed instrument that rests on the floor. The performer sits in a chair, the harp between its legs and plucks at the strings with its fingers.
help	/hɛlp/	Employees, the people who work in a place of business.

LEVEL II/III: AN /?/ & /h/ DIALOGUE: AMANDA & HUBERT

Hubert:	Anóther ápple tree?! Amánda, you are <u>óff your rócker</u>.
Amanda:	Hélp me, Húbert. The róot ball is héavy.
Hubert:	Hów can you búy so mány? We alréady have óver a húndred trées!
Amanda:	Húbert, I'm an ápple grówer. I have an <u>órchard</u>.
Hubert:	The expénse is kílling us.
Amanda:	What mákes my órchard spécial is the varíety of ápples I grów.
Hubert:	I understánd that, bút . . .
Amanda:	I have órders for the entíre crop of Wínesaps we plánted eight yéars agó.
Hubert:	Oh, all ríght. What kínd is thís one?
Amanda:	Thése. There are éighteen móre in the trúck.
Hubert:	Oh, my áching bánk bálance.

VOCABULARY

<u>óff your rócker</u>	/?⊃́f y⊃rákUr/	To be crazy.
<u>órchard</u>	/?⊃́rčUrd/	A farm of fruit or nut trees.

THE VOICELESS GLOTTAL FRICATIVE + BILABIAL GLIDE COMBINATION /hw/

/hw/ is one of the few Old English pronunciations to survive the changes that Norman French imposed.

/hw/ appears in words that begin with the ALPHABET LETTERS wh.

when where whíle why whale whíttle whímper whim

wharf wheel whiff whet whirl whit whorl whoop

white whískey whip whine whíther whérewithall

FIND /hw/ IN THIS RHYME

Whéther 'tis cóld or whéther 'tis hót,

There's góing to be wéather, líke it or nót.

A /hw/ NON-RHYMING RHYME

Whére is the whíte múlberry búsh,

Whén did you púll it out?

Why did you whíttle that múlberry wood?

You knów I wánted to dry it óut mysélf!

CHAPTER IV

Suprasegmentals

"Singing" in Standard American English or the Most Common Suprasegmental Patterns in American English

INTRODUCTION

Suprasegmentals are phonetic elements, combinations of sound features that work together to add meaning to phrases and sentences. 8 of the most important are

1) SYLLABLE STRESS 2) PHRASE ACCENT 3) PAUSE
4) MAINTAINING RISE 5) RISE-FALL/PITCH 6) RHYTHM/SYNCOPATION
7) SPEED 8) VOICE QUALITY

Together these sound features or suprasegmentals create INTONATION CONTOUR, the melodic line of a word, phrase or sentence.

Suprasegmentals help to make what is spoken easily understood.

Every language has its own suprasegmental patterns and intonation contours. The patterns that characterize one language are specific to that language only.

The suprasegmentals and intonation contours of English are specific to English. They are just as important to fluency in English as grammatical correctness and a large vocabulary.

1. SYLLABLE STRESS

English words with 2 or more syllables carry stress on the penultimate or next-to-the-last syllable. Syllable stress in English usually goes together with a rise in pitch. And an unstressed syllable often drops in pitch.

The 2 most common pitch patterns are

a. Raise your voice on the stressed syllable.
b. Drop your voice on the unstressed syllable.

1a. TWO-SYLLABLE WORDS

swéetie	báby	fínish	kítten
swí	bé	fÍ	kÍ
t	b	n	t
i	i	I	I
		š	n

1b. THREE-SYLLABLE WORDS

decíded	árgueing	divínely	precísion
sái	?ár	váin	sÍ
d	gyu	l	prI ž
dI I	w	dI i	I
d	i		n
	η		

1c. FOUR-SYLLABLE WORDS

préferably	consíderate
prɛ́	sÍ
fUr	dUr
ə	kən I
b	t
l	
i	

2. PHRASE ACCENT

English phrases can range in length from a single syllable, such as

Whát?

to that of several syllables, such as

A Nánking nánny námed Náncy.

In this text the vowels in pertinent syllables, single or larger, are marked with an accent. The reason is to help the student identify rises in pitch.

SINGLE WORDS/PHRASES

2a. Hélp!

é
h l
p
!

2b. Stóp!

á
st
p
!

2c. Wáit.

é
w
t
.

2d. No.

ó
n
o
.

NOTE: Once you combine more than one word in a single phrase, 3. PAUSE, 4. MAINTAINING RISE & 5. RISE-FALL/PITCH join in. See the rest of the examples in this chapter for further clarification.

SINGLE SYLLABLE-WORD PHRASES

2e. Sée the bée.

bí
sí í
ðə .

2f. In a mínute.

mÍ
ə n
In I
t
.

2g. Béat the héat.

hí
bít í
ðə t
.

2h. A bít of spít.

Í
bÍt sp
?ə əv t
.

3. PAUSE

Pauses between syllables in a word, between words and between phrases, are necessary for

a. catching one's breath,
b. helping one to articulate a sound or group of sounds more clearly,
c. give the listener a chance to understand what is being said, and
d. give the speaker time to find the words that would best express its thoughts.

3a. Héy, Wáyne, wáit!

wє́
wé
hé n t
!

3b. Bétter rést, Mél.

rє́st
mє́l.
tUr
bє́

4. MAINTAINING RISE

English helps the speaker make it clear to the listener that one is not yet done speaking. All one has to do is keep the pitch of one's voice high.

4a. Sám the Mán is on the lám.

lǽ
ðə
sǽm mǽn án m
Iz .
ðə

4b. Abel is báking a cake.

ké
békiŋ
?ébəl ə k
Iz .

4c. Pénny is a wét hen.

wέt
pέni h
yÍz ə ɛ
n
.

5. RISE-FALL/PITCH

In English statements, highest rises in pitch occur most often on the stressed syllable of the last word. Then there is an abrupt drop in pitch.

This English intonation contour pattern helps the listener to know when the speaker is finished speaking.

The examples above and those that follow, with their syllable stresses, phrase accents, pauses and maintaining rise intonation contours, illustrate how all of the suprasegmental elements, including the common pattern of rapid drop in pitch, work together.

5a. Nó, nó, Nanétte, nót nów.

nát
nó net n
nó a
næ u
.

5b. Néver néedle a nérvous pórcupine.

pɔ́r
nÚrvIs kyu
ní ə p
nɛ́vUr dəl a
i
n
.

5c. Mártha's cár is márvelous.

már
θəz ve
már karIz l
e
s
.

6. RHYTHM/SYNCOPATION

English rhythm is syncopated. That means it moves from

a. "stepping" on the downbeat to
b. emphasizing it by breaking up the rhythm into uneven segments by starting on the upbeat.

6a. Súmmer bréezes are sóft and wárm.

wɔ́
brí sɔ́ft r
sÁmUr zIz ænd m
*a*r .

ANALYSIS:

Súmmer and bréezes both begin on the downbeat, the syllable that carries stress. These syllables are longer than the unstressed syllables in each word.

The phrase are sóft and wárm begins before the downbeat: on the upbeat. This is because both are and and are unstressed syllables.

In other words, stressed syllables and accents on phrases are located on the downbeat which highlights them.

Unstressed syllables are located on the upbeat. Their job is to help emphasize stressed syllables and phrase accents.

6b. Ráiny days máke me crázy.

```
                          kré
                              z
réni         mék    mi          i
        dez                       .
```

6c. A búndle of únwashed únderwear.

```
                                 Ʌ́n
     bɅ́ndəl     Ʌ́n                 dUr
                     wašt
?ə         əv                          w
                                         e
                                          r
                                           .
```

6d. Bútton úp, Amánda.

```
            Ʌ́p
                      mæn
      tIn                    də.
    bɅ́            ?ə
```

7. SPEED

Speeding up and slowing down, is closely tied to rhythm, especially syncopation. In English it is pretty easy to know when to speed up and when to slow down.

Articles (a/an, the) and prepositions (in, of, under, over, from, to, behind, in front of) are speeded up.

Conjuctions (and, or, but) are given more time.

Prepositional phrases (a preposition + a noun phrase) illustrate both variations in speed and rhythm/syncopation.

A SIMPLE SENTENCE COMBINING THE ARTICLES a/an & the

7a. An ápple a dáy is the bést médicine.

bɛ́st
mɛ́
æpəl dé ðə dI
?æn ə yIz s
I
n
.

NOTE: American English favors syncopated rhythm in general, and rise-fall on the last phrase of a sentence. In careful speech pauses highlight syncopated rhythm.

CONJUNCTION EXAMPLES: <u>and, but, or</u>

7b. and thén . . . but nót untíl . . . or élse!

ɛ́
ðɛ́n nát l
tÍl s
?ænd bΛt ?Λn ?ↄr !

NOTE: NEGATIVES (not, never, nothing) and other QUALIFIERS (just, even so, mostly, very, some, a little) are emphasized and therefore rise in pitch.

PREPOSITION EXAMPLES: <u>in, of, on</u>

7c. in líne. of sómething. on a hígh.

lá sΛ́m há
i θ ə
n i i
?In . ?Λv η ?an .
.

7d. in a mínute. of the family.

mÍ fǽ
n m
I ə
?inə t ?Λvðə l
. i
.

8. VOICE QUALITY is a key suprasegmental element contributing to the kinds of meanings communicated.

a. A soft, relaxed, low-pitched voice allows the speaker to say <u>In a mínute</u> without causing offence.

b. At the other extreme, a tense, harsh, grating voice quality can make <u>Helló</u> sound offensive.

c. Flattening the intonation contour often gives the impression that the speaker is depressed, emotionally exhausted, or distancing itself from the conversation.

d. High pitch in conjunction with very fast enunciation can indicate nervousness, emotional upset, or fear.

4 COMMON SENTENCE INTONATION CONTOURS IN STANDARD AMERICAN ENGLISH

1. The Polite Question
2. The Command/Demand Question
3. The Polite Statement
4. The Impolite Statement

1. THE POLITE QUESTION

The polite question rises in shallow steps.

?
nie
Rón
rúnning,
you
are
1a. Whére

?
pea
Swéet
it,
ís
1b. Whát

?
hóurs
two
séventy-
for
míllion
twénty
me
lénd
you
1c. Cán

2. THE IMPOLITE COMMAND/DEMAND QUESTION

There are 2 command/demand questions types. Both identify the speaker as superior in rank and so, can dispense with courtesy.

a. is IMPOLITE. The sentence may have a question mark at the end, but the INTONATION CONTOUR is the same as that of IMPERATIVE sentence.
b. is somewhat more polite. It strikes the middle ground between the shallow rising steps of the polite question and the steep descending steps of the impolite statement.
c. Voice quality also contributes to the kinds of meanings communicated.

2a1. Whát
ís
it,
Swéet
pea
?

2b1. Whát

pea?

ís Swéet

it,

2a2. Whére

are

you

rún

ning,

Rón

nie

?

2b2. Whére ?

are nie

you Rón

rún

ning,

you

2a3. Cán lénd

me twénty séventy-

míllion for two

hó

urs

?

?
hó s
lénd míl two ur
me lion séventy-
you twénty for
2b3. Cán

2a4. Why
dóesn't
ányone
téll
me
ány
thing
!

téll
me
ány ány
2b4. Why dóesn't one thing!

3. THE POLITE STATEMENT

This statement-type sentence has an intonation contour which modulates. It rises, falls slightly or maintains rise, and has the usual steep rise-fall in pitch on the last phrase.

The polite statement commonly rises highest on adjectives, nouns, and main verbs.

Sentences consisting of single-syllable words illustrate the most common intonation contour pattern of American English in polite statements.

house built yé
3a. The was last a
r
.

cráck in the
cát slípped wá
3b. A thróugh the l
l
.

3c. Tím líkes skí yéar
ro
to u
n
d
.

THE COMPLEX VERB TENSES

Variations in intonation contour depend upon the speaker's intentions and feelings.

But there are certain structures in American English syntax that tend to push and pull certain suprasegmental features around.

Pitch, for example, usually rises on the main verb of a verb phrase.

But when a qualifier (some, many) or a negative (not, never) is inserted between the helping verb and the main verb, then both qualifier and negative tend to rise highest in pitch.

THE COMPLEX ACTIVE VERB TENSES:

A) 1. PAST 2. PRESENT 3. FUTURE CONTINUOUS/PROGRESSIVE

BE + MAIN VERB + ING

B) 1. PRESENT 2. PAST PERFECT

HAVE/HAD + MAIN VERB

C) 1. PRESENT 2. PAST PERFECT CONTINUOUS

HAVE/HAD + BEEN + MAIN VERB +ING

NOTE: Pause, rhythm/syncopation, maintaining rise, and rise-fall work together with rises in pitch. All are equally critical to American English intonation contours.

A) 1. PAST CONTINUOUS/PROGRESSIVE: BE + MAIN VERB + ING

1a. I was góing for a wálk, when it stárted to ráin.

1b. Jóan was flying her Céssna last níght.

1c. Fréd was rúnning in the Néw York Márathon last mónth.

A) 2. PRESENT CONTINUOUS/PROGRESSIVE: <u>BE + MAIN VERB + ING</u>

2a. My síster Kínsey <u>is</u> <u>wórking</u> for IBM now.

2b. The Whíte House <u>is</u> <u>sénding</u> us a spéker.

2c. Yés, it's trúe. <u>I'm</u> <u>rúnning</u> for Président.

góing á
búy hóuse l
2d. Théy're to that áfter l
.

A) 3. FUTURE CONTINUOUS/PROGRESSIVE: (BE) + MAIN VERB + ING

Sún
méeting pá d
my rents on a
3a. You will be y
.

wéd
bé lót of d
a fóod i
3b. There'll the n
at g
.

3c. You'll be nót drí ving the cár to n í g h t .

3d. We'll be bícycling to séna Kis Párk in an hó u r .

B) 1. PRESENT PERFECT: HAVE + MAIN VERB

1a. We have hád a núm ber of wínning lót te ry tí ck e t s .

1b. Have you hád bréakfast yét?

1c. I háven't had a chánce to páy the gás bill this mónth.

1d. My hóuse hasn't been páinted in yéars.

1e. She has óften rún in the Bóston Márathon.

Móun
t
Húnter a
cíded skí at i
1f. We de to n
have .

alréady Tímes
réad the this
1g. I've mór
n
i
n
g
.

B) 2. PAST PERFECT: HAD + MAIN VERB

fó
Vá púr rúnning r
chased shoes be e
2a. lerie had .

spéech

réady

stúdents régistered c

had al for the l

2b. The a

s

s

.

C) 1. PRESENT PERFECT CONTINUOUS HAS/HAVE + BEEN + MAIN VERB +ING

éx dáy twó

ercising hóur a for mó

1a. Wé an n

have been t

h

s

.

síng sínce she was

ing thré

1b. Annétte e

has been .

plúmb áll
er wórk d
1c. That has been ing á
y
.

sléeping 9:00 p.m. ní
síonce last g
1d. Théy have been h
t
.

C) 2. PAST PERFECT CONTINUOUS HAD + BEEN + MAIN VERB +ING

háving dréadful Márjorie
2a. I day when arríved to
had been a

chéer me
ú
p
.

páinting twénty
for néarly years
2b. Géorgia Kéeffe
had been
O'

pér Tá Mé
móving manently os, New x
befóre to i
c
o
.

INTONATION CONTOUR CHANGES

SYLLABLES

When in polite statements nouns have 2 or more syllables and adjectives and qualifiers (very, a lot) are added, then the intonation contour changes.

This occurs because of the increase in the number of syllables, and because adjectives, adverbs, modals and other modifiers change the meaning of a phrase.

Changes in meaning, and variations in number of syllables per phrase, lead to changes in the shape of a sentence's intonation contour.

ló twó
yéllow co nial búilt yéars
1. The was a
g
ó
.

cráck wá
tábby slíp in the l
cát ping thróugh a l
2. A is .

ál
3. Tímothy ways líked skí Ás
Jónes to in p
e
n
.

swé
óverripe véry véry e
ápple sóur t
4. An can táste or .

B. Unlike other nouns, subject pronouns do not rise in pitch in polite statements. (They do in Spanish).

But qualifiers of quantity (all, some) and qualifiers of time (soon, sometimes) do go up in pitch, especially when they appear at the beginning of a phrase.

áll
líkes skí ye
1. She to ar
ro
u
n
d
.

lót
dríve
a wárm
2. We in wéa
th
e
r
.

réally
lóve pár
thrówing big t
3. They i
e
s
.

C. Whenever the speaker raises the pitch of a modal (must, may, might, could, would, should) higher than the main verb, the speaker is insisting the listener drop everything and listen.

The sentence is no longer polite.

1. You múst vísit us when éver you're in tówn.

2. We shóuld have gone shópping éarlier.

3. They cóuldn't live in that hóuse any lónger.

THE POSSESSIVE PRONOUNS

MY/MINE, YOUR/YOURS, HER/HERS, HIS, OUR/OURS, THEIR/THEIRS

D. These pronouns act as adjectives to nouns in noun phrases. They are rarely highlighted in polite statements.

1. <u>My</u> hóuse was búilt last yéar.

2. <u>Our</u> yéllow colónial was búilt twó yéars agó.

3. <u>Your</u> cár is óver héating.

párties gréat

4. <u>Their</u> are f

u

n

.

évery

fór vísits súm

to <u>her</u> m

5. <u>We</u> look ward e

r

.

thé

hóuse córner i

on the r

6. That is s

.

E. In nearly every language, including English, imperative statements usually begin with a verb. The subject pronoun or noun is absent structurally (in the structure of the sentence), but it is understood to be present semantically (as part of the meaning of the sentence).

Command/demand imperatives express the speaker's superiority. The statement is a command others are expected to obey without question.

The intonation contour moves from high to low in steep steps.

1. Come
hére,
chíl
d
r
e
n
.

2. Dón't
tóu
ch
the
wál
l
s
.

3. Gíve
me
a há
n
d,
Pé
t
e
r
.

4. Stóp
th
á
t
!

5. Gó
to
sléep
n
ó
w
.

6. Gét
me
a
gláss
of
té
a
.

7. Sít
d
ó
w
n
.

8. Dón't
sit
in
that
chá
i
r
.

POLITE IMPERATIVES

F. It is possible to articulate an imperative statement politely by using polite sentence intonation contours.

1. Come
hé
re,
chíld
ren.

2. Dón't
yél
l
so
mú
c
h
.

3. Sít down in that chá ir. 4. Be líeve me, it's trú e.

G. CONTRASTS BETWEEN A. COMMAND/DEMAND & F. POLITE IMPERATIVES

1a. Cóme up and sée me sóme time.

The great comedian, MAE WEST, was famous for her polite imperatives.

1f. Cóme up and sée me sómeti m e.

2a. Léave I'm
n tí
ó r
w, e
G d
e .
o
r
g
e
.

nów, ge. tí
or r
2f. Léave Ge I'm e
d
.

APPENDIX I

A List of Suggested Songs

A–L

A YOU'RE ADORABLE
AIN'T MISBEHAVIN'
AIN'T SHE SWEET
AND THE BAND PLAYED ON
THE ANIMAL FAIR
THE ANNIVERSARY WALTZ
AS TIME GOES BY
BABY FACE
BALLIN' THE JACK
BEI MIR BIST DU SCHÖN
THE BEST THINGS IN LIFE ARE FREE
THE BIG ROCK CANDY MOUNTAIN
BILL BAILEY
BLUE TAIL FLY
BROTHER, CAN YOU SPARE A DIME?
BUFFALO GALS
BY THE LIGHT OF THE SILVERY MOON
CALIFORNIA, HERE I COME
BYE, BYE, BLACKBIRD
CRAZY RHYTHM
DAISY BELL / THE SIDEWALKS OF NEW YORK (same melody)
THE ERIE CANAL
FIVE FOOT TWO, EYES OF BLUE
FORTY-SECOND STREET
GET HAPPY
GIVE MY REGARDS TO BROADWAY
HEART OF MY HEART
HE FLOATS THROUGH THE AIR
I CAN'T GIVE YOU ANYTHING BUT LOVE, BABY
IF YOU KNEW SUSIE
I'M A YANKEE DOODLE DANDY
I'M JUST WILD ABOUT HARRY
I'M LOOKING OVER A FOUR-LEAF CLOVER
IN THE GOOD OLD SUMMERTIME
IT AIN'T GONNA RAIN NO MORE
IT TAKES A WORRIED MAN
I'VE BEEN WORKING ON THE RAILROAD
JEEPERS CREEPERS
JUST A SONG AT TWILIGHT
LET ME CALL YOUR SWEETHEART
LITTLE BROWN JUG

M–Z

MA, HE'S MAKING EYES AT ME
MACK THE KNIFE
MARGIE
ME AND MY GAL
MEET ME IN ST. LOUIS, LOUIS
THE MIDNIGHT SPECIAL
MOONLIGHT BAY
MY BABY JUST CARES FOR ME
MY WILD IRISH ROSE
OH! YOU BEAUTIFUL DOLL
O! THEM GOLDEN SLIPPERS
THE OLD GREY/GRAY MARE
ONE MEATBALL
ON THE SUNNY SIDE OF THE STREET
POPEYE THE SAILOR MAN
RYE WHISKEY
SCARBOROUGH FAIR
SECOND-HAND ROSE
SIDE BY SIDE
THE SIDEWALKS OF NEW YORK
SING, EVERYONE, SING
STARDUST
SUGAR BLUES
SWANEE
SWEET BETSY FROM PIKE
SWEET GEORGIA BROWN
SUMMERTIME
TEA FOR TWO
TELL ME A STORY
'WAY DOWN YONDER IN NEW ORLEANS
WHEN MY SUGAR WALKS DOWN THE STREET
WHEN THE RED, RED ROBIN COMES BOB, BOBBIN' ALONG
THE WIZARD OF OZ
WHO THREW THE OVERALLS IN MISTRESS MURPHY'S CHOWDER?
YES, WE HAVE NO BANANAS
YOU ARE MY SUNSHINE
YOU'RE DRIVING ME CRAZY
YOU'RE THE CREAM IN MY COFFEE
ZIPPITY DOO DAH, ZIPPITY YAY